Proposal

Production Automation
3160 De La Cruz Blvd., Suite 210
Santa Clara, CA 95054

Japanese
Manufacturing
Techniques

JAPANESE MANUFACTURING TECHNIQUES

Nine Hidden Lessons in Simplicity

RICHARD J. SCHONBERGER

THE FREE PRESS
A Division of Macmillan Publishing Co., Inc.
NEW YORK

Collier Macmillan Publishers
LONDON

The Free Press
A Division of Macmillan Publishing Co., Inc.
866 Third Avenue, New York, N.Y. 10022

Collier Macmillan Canada, Inc.

Printed in the United States of America

printing number
5 6 7 8 9 10

Library of Congress Cataloging in Publication Data

Schonberger, Richard J.
    Japanese manufacturing techniques.

    Bibliography: p.
    Includes index.
    1. Industrial management—Japan. 2. Production
management. I. Title.
HD70.J3S36   1982   658.5′00952   82-48495
ISBN 0-02-929100-3

Contents

Contents

Preface

Some seem to believe that we now know all there is to know about Japanese industrial management, productivity, and quality; that we have raked the Japanese system over the coals and carefully examined the ashes. The truth is that the West has hardly begun to understand Japanese success factors, and much of what is professed in current readings consists of half-truths and misconceptions that stand in the way of rapid progress in catching up with the Japanese. As McGill notes, the popular books about Japanese management (at least three have been best-sellers) "have little to say about life in the corporate trenches. Their message comes from and is addressed to CEOs [chief executive officers] and members of boards . . . little is said [about what] managers in the middle" are to do.[1]

This book deals with what managers in the middle are to do and at the same time addresses broad concepts and issues that are relevant to top managers. And there is a good deal to say: nine lessons in simplicity, each the central topic of one full chapter. Japanese manufacturers have rejected our complex management prescriptions—our obsession with programs, with controls, with computers and information processing, with behavioral interventions, and with mathematical modeling. Instead of developing complex solutions, the Japanese way is to simplify the problem. Among the simplifiers, Toyota is the standard-bearer. The simple but ingenious production management and quality control approaches developed by Toyota and other leading manufacturers seem to travel easily to other Japanese firms without really being taught in Japanese business schools or promoted by consultants.

I believe that the approaches travel easily to other countries as well. The inherent good sense of the techniques and ap-

proaches themselves fosters their mobility. And there is prelimi-
nary evidence, from Japanese subsidiaries operating on U.S.
shores, that Japanese production and quality management works
in non-Japanese settings. With apologies to Jacques Brel, Japanese systems are alive and well and operating in the United
States.

Roots of the Japanese System

The system of production and quality management that the Japanese have developed has cultural roots. That is, Japanese social
behavioral tendencies, which are products of the unique Japanese
environment, have accommodated development of highly effective production systems. But the systems themselves consist of
simple procedures and techniques, most of which do not require
a particular environment or cultural setting for their implementation. (Throughout history good ideas that have sprung forth from
a given set of circumstances have been adopted elsewhere as fast
as the word could spread.)

The System's Main Concerns

The Japanese system consists essentially of two types of procedures and techniques. The two types pertain to: (1) productivity;
(2) quality. The aspect of the Japanese system dealing most directly with productivity is known as the *just-in-time system.* Just-
in-time directly addresses the material cost component of productivity. The indirect effects are even more pronounced, affecting
elements of productivity from scrap to worker motivation to process yield. Japanese quality improvement is partially addressed
by just-in-time, but there are a host of other Japanese quality
improvement concepts and procedures as well. A term that is
often used in Japan to describe the set of Japanese quality improvement procedures is *total quality control,* which in turn en-

compasses some of the just-in-time techniques, and improves productivity through avoidance of waste. In other words, just-in-time and total quality control overlap, and they will be introduced together in an early chapter, in which their central role in the Japanese strategy of market dominance is demonstrated. Separable just-in-time and total quality control issues will be treated in more detail in later chapters. The lessons in these detailed chapters show how simple techniques beget more of the same, encompassing most of the manufacturing environment: plant configurations, development and care of equipment, material control and handling, scheduling, engineering, human relationships, and supplier relationships.

Specialists

Just-in-time and total quality control procedures are not the purview of white-collar staff advisers and specialists. As other authors have noted, the Japanese rely little on staff specialists. The worker and the line managers are the focal point, and innovations concerning productivity and quality improvement are nurtured on the shop floor, not in someone's office. The Japanese subsidiaries in the United States, however, find themselves with managers and professionals educated in specialist-oriented American colleges, and most have prior experience as specialists in traditional American industrial environments. Some of the Japanese subsidiaries have found ways to dampen the specialist orientation —or to redirect the specialist's efforts toward more general plant objectives—and thus overcome the chief obstacle to making Japanese systems work in Western industry.

Implementation in the West

Otherwise well-informed Western readers may be exposed to a new world of management ideas in this book. Some of the ideas that have been spreading in North America have done so in about the same ways that they spread in Japan: among the lower and middle managers. Just-in-time has been a hot topic at their professional association meetings in the past year or so. *Implementation* of these ideas has not made much progress—and cannot as long as upper managers and their consultants and advisers remain uninformed about the power of Japanese just-in-time production and total quality control. The purposes of this book are to be broadly informative as well as to show how the system can be put into effect at the operating level.

Because implementation has been slow, in this book I will sometimes be unable to cite plants in this country that have adopted a particular element of the Japanese system being discussed—but it is only a matter of time before this will change. We will learn and we will implement the system of the Japanese, because their production and quality procedures are the best in the world. The American system was the standard of excellence in a previous era, and other countries, including Japan, studied it and used it. The world's countries learn from each other in a never-ending cycle. And it's healthy.

Acknowledgments

There are a number of individuals and organizations that contributed information and inspiration helpful to me in writing this book. Robert Hall of Indiana University and the Repetitive Manufacturing Group of the American Production and Inventory Control Society were ahead of almost everyone else in North America in trying to understand Japanese systems, and my association with the Group has been fruitful. Robert H. Hayes of the Harvard Business School read the manuscript and contributed particularly valuable suggestions, as well as providing helpful case information on Sanyo, U.S.A. William Harahan, director of manufacturing planning at Ford Motor Co., also read the manuscript and steered me away from several dubious assumptions. Ed Hay of Fram Corp. was one of the first American visitors to Japanese industry who really learned what the Toyota system is all about, and I have been a note-taking demon in Ed's presentations. Leighton Smith, Masakatsu Mori, and several others who were in Arthur Andersen and Co.'s Tokyo offices have spread the message of Japanese productivity and quality at professional development meetings around this country, some of which I have been fortunate enough to sit in on.

Japanese companies in Japan and their U.S. subsidiaries have been most cooperative. I owe special thanks to Kichiro Ando, Doug Sutton, and Bob Johnson of Kawasaki, U.S.A.; Dennis Butt, Jerry Claunch, and Bob Summers, formerly with Kawasaki; Jim Keller of TRI-CON Industries (U.S. subsidiary of Tokyo Seating Co.); Mike Kreglow of Honda, U.S.A.; Mike Morimoto and Richard Getty of Sony, U.S.A.; Yancy Fukagawa of Matsushita, U.S.A.; Kentaro Arai of Calsonic, Inc., and Nihon Radiator Co., Japan; Larry Herold of Sanyo, U.S.A.; Hiroshi Suginuma, Michio Tani, Ichiro Tamura, and Fumiaki Amae of

Kawasaki, Japan; Koichi Yamada, T. Kontani, and H. Sakaki-bara of Matsushita Electric Co., Japan; President Hisakichi Ohta, S. Kawanabe, Tadashi Odate, and Shinji Komatsu of Nihon Radiator Co., Japan, and Mr. Takashige Yamane of Mitsuboshi Belting Co., Japan.

Finally, I owe thanks to Sang Lee and Gary Schwendiman of the University of Nebraska for organizing the Japan-United States Business Conference, which brought together Japanese and American industrial and academic authorities on Japanese production systems, and to Joyce Anderson, Jane Chrastil, Cindy LeGrande, and Angela Sullivan for their patience in working on my manuscript.

CHAPTER 1

Industrial Management in Japan and the World

LESSON 1: Management technology is a highly transportable commodity.

I was sitting on a bar stool at the Hyatt Regency O'Hare, Chicago. I was to speak on Japanese manufacturing management at the National Assembly Engineering Conference the next day. A man sat down at the next stool and we struck up a conversation. He was an industrial salesman passing through town and was inquisitive about the conference and my role in it. He wanted my views on the Japanese success formula, and I said that it is inventory control. Lest I should appear ridiculous, I hastened to explain:

"The Japanese have a "just-in-time" production objective. They use engineering to drastically cut machine setup times so that it is economical to run very small batches. The ideal is to make one piece just in time for the next operation. In management terms, the economic order quantity has been cut down to approach one. Do you understand about EOQs?"

He did, and I continued. "The advantage may seem small—

1

some savings on inventory carrying costs, since you produce and carry smaller lots. But the Japanese have found that the main benefits are in quality, worker motivation, and productivity. Here's how it works.

"Say that a worker makes one piece and hands it to a second worker whose job is to join another piece to it; but the second worker can't make them fit, because the first worker made a defective part. The second worker wants to meet his quota and doesn't like being stopped, so he lets the first worker know about it right away. The first worker's reactions are predictable: He tries not to foul up again—and tries to root out the problem that caused the defective part.

"The typical Western way, by contrast, is to make parts in large lots. A whole forklift-truck load—two weeks' worth, maybe. The second worker might find 10 percent to be defective, but he doesn't care. He just tosses a defective part into a scrap or rework bin and grabs another. There are enough good ones to keep him busy, so why complain about defectives?

"So you see, the Japanese cut the wasted hours and wasted materials by not allowing large lots of defectives to be produced. The main force that drives Japanese quality and productivity is just-in-time inventory control."

"Is it that simple?" asked the salesman.

"It's that simple," I answered.

Of course, I overstated my case. The Japanese have a well-oiled national economic machine that runs on hard work, dedication, frugality, national resolve, and other factors. Furthermore, Japanese excellence in quality control stems not just from small lot sizes and quick discovery of defects, but, more importantly, from an industry-wide assault upon bad quality that has been going on since 1949. The Japanese have translated their quality control aspirations into a collection of procedures and techniques that may be labeled *total quality control* (TQC).

Total quality control procedures, implemented in concert with the just-in-time (JIT) system and a host of related productivity enhancing techniques, give Japan a decisive edge in industrial *management*. Catching up with the Japanese depends not so much on changing tax, trade, regulatory, and labor laws and policies as it does on changing our industrial management policies, procedures, and systems. Happily, most management concepts and approaches are readily transportable, and the basic simplicity and logic of JIT and TQC enhance their transportability from Japan to industry in America and the West generally.

The purpose of this book is to tell the heretofore untold story of Japanese just-in-time manufacturing control and total quality control and of a few early, successful attempts at implementing JIT/TQC in American plants. JIT/TQC is a multifaceted manufacturing management system, and several chapters are needed to examine each facet. A good place to begin is with the natural question "How did the Japanese develop JIT/TQC?"

The Genesis of JIT/TQC

With all of the recent journalistic attention given to Japanese industry, most of us know by now that Japan is small, crowded, and resource-poor. Nearly 125 million people inhabit the Japanese islands, whose land mass is about the same as Montana's. Montana is rich in natural resources, however, compared with Japan. The combination of masses of human resources with few natural resources may help to explain Japanese resourcefulness. The Japanese make do with little and avoid waste. The modern Japanese system of factory management—the just-in-time approach, featuring hand-to-mouth management of materials, with total quality control—seems in character with their historical penchant to conserve. To the Japanese factory worker, JIT/TQC objectives should seem reasonable, proper, and easy to accept, inasmuch as JIT/TQC attempts to control such costly sources of waste as:

- Idle inventories, which constitute waste of scarce material resources, and, indirectly, energy for basic material conversion and refining.

- Storage of idle inventories, which wastes limited space.

- Defective parts, subassemblies, and final products, which are a waste of materials/energy.

A Throw-away Society

In contrast to Japan, Western countries, especially those in North America, have had abundant space, energy, and material resources. High-performing manufacturing companies learned to cultivate consumer demand for change and variety and to hold goods and parts in inventory in order to be responsive to changing consumer demand. In the previous era of low interest rates, cheap materials, and plentiful storage space, the strategy was affordable. As Western consumers became more accustomed to annual style changes and "planned obsolescence," a "throw-away society" replaced earlier generations of careful quality-conscious buyers. The industrial engine ran on the talents of designers, packagers, and advertisers. Turning out new goods quickly and keeping well-stocked shelves of finished goods and components became a path toward profitability. Waste in the form of defective parts, or shelves full of "passable" ones, was not a dominant concern.

Consumptive, profligate habits probably grew in America and Canada roughly in parallel with the growth of a middle class. The trend was interrupted during the World War II years when the countries needed—and got—reliable war supplies and equipment. Following the war, the growth of middle-class consumerism was rapid. The trend would surely have continued unabated had not the OPEC-induced oil shock of 1973, as well as the raw material shortages beginning about 1971, occurred.

4

Oil Shock

The fivefold rise in the price of crude oil between 1970 and 1974 led to worldwide economic travail. The primary effects—skyrocketing costs for petroleum as a fuel for heating and for running automotive and other engines—were bad enough. But the high cost and scarcities of petroleum products had numerous secondary effects, especially in high-energy-using material processing industries, like aluminum, plastics, copper, and steel—from which much of the world's durable goods are made. Acute shortages of basic materials plagued industrial buyers, and the costs of these materials leaped upward.

The industrial world became resigned to elevated costs of materials, and many companies perceived the need to be more resourceful. The good old days were gone. Industry began to warm to the task of overhauling its materials management procedures—and, for that matter, its plant and equipment, its product designs, its manufacturing controls, and its human resource management approaches, all of which affect the quantities of materials bought, used, stored, and sold.

Somehow the Japanese took the task more seriously than did the rest of the world. According to Dansby, Japanese ideas on tighter material control began to be implemented in earnest right after the 1973 oil shock.[1] The reason for the quick reaction may have something to do with a lack of alternatives: Since Japan relies upon imported energy and materials for nearly all of its needs, better management of these imported resources is perhaps the only viable option for coping with runaway costs.

While Japanese industry was perfecting just-in-time materials management and factory control, the West searched for political and economic solutions to the energy/material cost dilemma. OPEC had to be pressured, the oil companies had to be watched, consumers had to conserve energy, and government had to tinker with taxes, tariffs, and quotas.

5

Western industry (oil companies excepted) was generally not blamed, implicated, or challenged—until the results of the Japanese effort to streamline factory management began to pinch unmercifully. It gradually became clear that the Japanese were not grabbing world market share—in autos, cameras, TVs, steel, shipbuilding, machine tools, and so forth—by dumping (i.e., by selling at below cost in export markets). The success was genuine, and the reasons were excellent product quality and phenomenal rates of productivity improvement. Among nations, Japan seemed most susceptible to economic damage from the world energy crisis, but Japan dramatically gained economic ground rather than losing it.

Improvement of the Quality Image

While the oil shock may have helped trigger Japanese development of just-in-time production management, the seeds of Japanese export success had been sown much earlier. Those of us who are old enough recall when the quality of Japanese export goods had as poor an image as any in the world. The Japanese knew it and were determined to do something about it in the post–World War II industrial rebuilding era.

A milestone year for quality control in Japan was 1949. The Japanese Union of Scientists and Engineers (JUSE) established a QC Research Group, and JUSE, together with the Japanese Standards Association (JSA), sponsored quality control seminars and launched two QC journals. Invitations went out to American QC leaders, Dr. W. E. Deming in 1950 and Dr. J. M. Juran in 1954, to lecture in Japan, and their visits are widely considered to have been highly influential.

Initially, the QC training efforts were concentrated on higher managers and on engineers. In 1960 the focus shifted to foremen: *QC Text for Foremen,* a two-volume set, was published by JUSE. In 1962 a periodical, *Gemba To QC* (QC for Foremen), was initi-

6

ated. The periodical, renamed *FQC* in 1973, had a monthly circulation of 93,000 in 1981.

Becoming aware, getting organized, and implementing Western quality control techniques (chiefly statistical sampling) constitute the thrust of the first fifteen years of quality control emphasis in Japan. Today, after years of intensive company-wide emphasis on quality control, Japanese quality control encompasses nearly every concept and approach known to the West—and a good deal more. Japanese total quality control particularly emphasizes:

1. A goal of continual quality improvement, project after project (rejection of the Western notion of an "acceptable quality level").

2. Worker (not QC department) responsibility.

3. Quality control of every process, not reliance upon inspection of lots for only selected processes (defect *prevention,* not random detection).

4. Measures of quality that are visible, visual, simple, and understandable, even to the casual observer.

5. Automatic quality measurement devices (self-developed).

So successful have the Japanese become in pursuing total quality control that many Japanese manufacturers now speak of attained quality levels measured in parts (defectives) per million, whereas Western norms have traditionally been measurable in parts per hundred, i.e., in percentages.

Industrial Management Expertise

While JIT and TQC were being perfected in Japan, management was not standing still elsewhere. Indeed, U.S. industry was

7

caught up in a major advance in production and inventory management—known as material requirements planning (MRP), a sophisticated computer-based system. A time-line analysis of the growth of industrial management expertise may help show where the world's industries learned what they know about producing goods, and where Japanese JIT/TQC and American MRP fit in.

The Industrial Revolution

Figure 1-1 traces some of the key developments in the history of the factory system and factory management. The industrial revolution, dating back to the mid-1700s, spawned the factory system itself, along with a multitude of inventions. The hallmark of the factory system is efficiency, which is attained by division of labor, interchangeable parts, and high volume (economies of scale). Skilled craftsmanship gave way to unskilled and semi-skilled factory workmanship, first in Europe and then in North America.

Eli Whitney, an American, contributed the idea of interchangeable parts—and attendant improvements in dependability, reliability, serviceability, and productive efficiency. Standardized designs for component parts gave rise to the need to manage work-in-process (WIP) inventories of parts (in addition to inventories of finished goods and raw materials); the cost and bother of planning for and controlling WIP inventories may be offset by faster deliveries, since the product is carried in a state of partial completion before the customer orders it.

Thanks to Whitney and scores of other innovative Americans during the industrial revolution, industrial management expertise in the New World probably equaled that of Europe by the end of the nineteenth century. Then, in the first half of this century, U.S. productivity outstripped the rest of the world. As is suggested in Figure 1-1, scientific management (SM) was the major advance in industrial management during this period, and SM was developed in the United States. While historians seem generally

8

Figure 1–1. Development of Manufacturing Management Expertise

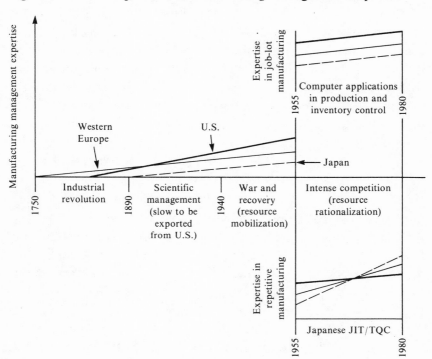

to think of the industrial revolution as having run its course by the turn of the present century, I like to think of scientific management as a continuation. Factory efficiency had been enhanced by standardization of product design, component parts, and tools, and by the widespread use of standard engine-driven machine tools. What remained nonstandardized was the labor component. For lack of a better way, carrot-and-stick (mostly stick) foremanship continued to be the chief means of controlling the undisciplined work force.

Scientific Management

Scientific management provided a better way. Frederick W. Taylor, Frank and Lillian Gilbreth, and a host of other pioneers of scientific management perfected work-study techniques so that the worker's task could be standardized. In work study, first the work method is improved—made simpler to do as well as more efficient; second, the improved method is timed, which provides the time standard; third, workers are trained in the standard method; and fourth, jobs are scheduled, supervised, and controlled with reference to the standard method and time. With scientific management, factory standardization was complete, and the implicit goals of the industrial revolution had finally been accomplished.

By the 1920s in the United States, the industrial engineering profession (which splintered off from mechanical engineering—the machine-tool experts) was well established as the duly vested purveyor of scientific management. Industrial engineers could be found plying their trade in factories from coast to coast. It took at least twenty years for Europe to learn about and adopt work study, and perhaps that time lag provides a good share of the explanation for American industrial supremacy in the world in the thirties, forties, and fifties.

I'll not attempt to trace the growth of Japanese industrial management expertise through midcentury. Suffice it to say that Japan lagged behind Europe and North America, but moved ahead of the rest of the world. For the time being let us skip quickly through the World War II and the war recovery years (more will be said in later chapters about management advances in those years). We move up to about 1955 on the time line of Figure 1-1, a time in which the industrial emphasis was shifting from resource mobilization to rationalization, i.e., efficient resource usage. At that point the time line splits into an upper and a lower segment. The upper segment highlights job-lot-manufacturing management, and the lower segment focuses on repetitive manufacturing management.

Job-Lot and Repetitive Production Management

It is common knowledge that Japan has moved to the top of the ladder in production of autos, cameras, consumer electronics items, and a host of other high-volume *repetitively* produced goods. Repetitive manufacturing is the industrial setting in which Japanese just-in-time production and total quality control thrive.

The general public is largely unaware that U.S. industry has become highly proficient in job-lot-manufacturing management in the last twenty years. While repetitive manufacturing is high-volume production of a narrow product line, job-lot manufacturing is medium- to low-volume production of a wide variety of products and models. The job-lot manufacturer must be able to react fast to a hard-to-predict and changeable mix of orders. A small change at the end-product level has ripple effects upon work in process all the way back through parts and raw material ordering, and keeping all of the ordering up to date used to be a data processing nightmare. But the United States is the world's leader in computer processing proficiency, and it was natural for computers to be harnessed to handle these data processing chores in job-lot manufacturing. A comprehensive computer-based manufacturing management system known as material requirements planning (MRP) was developed in the United States in the 1960s and spread throughout U.S. industry in the 1970s. MRP has not proven to be as momentous a leap forward as was scientific management, but there are some similarities: Both SM and MRP are strictly American innovations; and despite vastly improved worldwide communications networks, MRP has been slow to cross the oceans—as was the case with SM.

Thus, the state of the art in industrial management today is roughly as is shown at the right in Figure 1-1. The United States is most proficient in job-lot-manufacturing management because MRP was invented and nurtured here. Japan is most proficient in repetitive manufacturing management because the just-in-time system was developed there. European industry employs little MRP or JIT but has a diversity of other management strengths. (Placement of European industry in "second place" on both scales in Figure 1-1 is based on an admittedly small amount of hard information.)[2]

The Just-in-Time Challenge

Those of us who have played some role in the MRP crusade[3] of
the 1970s may feel justifiably proud. One may even be tempted to
rationalize that perhaps U.S. industry should attempt to build up
its MRP-controlled job-lot industries and more or less abandon
repetitive manufacturing industries and JIT management to the
Japanese. Such rationalization would be shallow. There are several reasons why Western manufacturers, including successful
job-lot MRP users, should learn all they can about Japanese JIT/
TQC:

1. The Japanese giants used to be job-lot producers, too.
They got to be giants not by catering to consumer whims but by
producing a few models very well, often in market segments that
were being ignored by other companies. Low-cost, high-quality
production leads to growth in market share (Henry Ford's credo).
With more market share—more volume—the plant moves toward long production runs, year-round repetitive production for
some product models. As we shall see in later chapters, repetitive
operations make it possible to tighten JIT inventory control still
more, which leads to still better quality and higher productivity.
Soon the product is so good that it becomes attractive not just to
shoppers who must economize but to all income levels including
the wealthy. At that point Western manufacturers that have tried
to compete by offering variety will have been pushed out of much
of the market.

2. Growth spawns variety. The company that has gotten
rich making "basic black" will then build a plant to make some
other model or product. Over time, the company ends up with a
full line of models, all produced and sold in volume and manufactured more or less repetitively—the present situation at Nissan,
Sony, Canon, and other top Japanese companies. The Western
job-lot competitor no longer has even the advantage of more
product variations.

12

3. Even manufacturers who are locked into a job-lot future can gain some quick benefits from JIT. Plants (or shops within plants) that produce a wide variety of parts generally try to batch several orders for the same part so that there can be one setup and one long production run. The idea is to avoid having to set up for several smaller runs spaced out over time, and there is sound economic wisdom in this—the economic order quantity (EOQ) concept. However, the Japanese have made us aware of the important benefits (never included in EOQ calculations) of smaller lots and smaller inventories: namely, better quality, less waste and rework, more awareness of sources of delay and error, higher levels of worker motivation, and greater process yield and productivity. You don't have to achieve one-at-a-time production to gain some of these JIT benefits; any move *toward* smaller lots will help.

4. Western job-lot manufacturers that have developed advanced computer-based MRP systems (advanced "closed-loop" MRP is coming to be called "MRP II") have an Achilles heel: quality. No quality control module has been developed to dovetail with MRP. Japan has much to learn about MRP; likewise Western MRP users have much to learn from Japan about total quality control.

5. Like all good management approaches, JIT/TQC requires hard work and discipline. But most management approaches are closed-ended; i.e., implementation (including debugging) is followed by a one-time boost in productivity. MRP is generally that way. (Or various MRP features can be implemented, one at a time, each capable of pushing up productivity a bit more.) The real power of JIT/TQC is that it has amplification properties. A round of JIT/TQC improvements tends to trigger another round, and another, and so on. In the next chapter the just-in-time chain reaction and its self-sustaining nature, coupled with total quality control, is closely examined. In later chapters we shall probe the elements of TQC and in the JIT causal chain, and consider some related issues. Three key issues are:

a. *Temperament.* The individualistic "every man for himself" temperament of workers in many Western countries, chiefly the United States, contrasts sharply with Japanese cooperation, dedication, harmony, and group-think decision processes. Can JIT systems, which forge closer bonds between workers by closing the time (inventory) gaps between them, work in a more individualistic setting?

b. *Geography.* In Japan suppliers can make deliveries in small quantities daily or more often because shipping distances are not a problem. How can just-in-time deliveries of raw materials and purchased parts be feasible given the vast shipping distances in countries like the United States?

c. *Education and training.* Japan has been immersed in quality control training for over 30 years. Is there any hope of catching up?

These and many other issues are addressed in the remaining chapters, and the answers are, for the most part, positive and optimistic. If the Japanese system can be studied as a collection of integrated techniques—and it surely can be, as it is in this book—then there is no reason not to be optimistic. Techniques travel well. Or, to put it in the form of a restatement of the first lesson:

The Japanese have had little trouble learning our techniques, and we will have little trouble learning theirs.

CHAPTER 2

Just-in-Time Production with Total Quality Control

LESSON 2: Just-in-time production exposes problems otherwise hidden by excess inventories and staff.

Western industry has amassed numerous prescriptions for catching up with the Japanese. Until recently, most prescription lists omitted Japanese just-in-time (JIT) production management and total quality control (TQC). Just-in-time production is simple, requires little use of computers, and in some industries can provide far tighter controls on inventory than are attainable through U.S. computer-based approaches. Furthermore, JIT leads to significantly higher quality and productivity, and provides visibility for results so that worker responsibility and commitment are improved. Applications and benefits of JIT/TQC may be extended from the factory itself forward into distribution and backward to the supplier end of the business. Total quality control is highly effective by itself, and the combination of JIT and TQC marshals a rate of productivity and quality improvement that demoralizes foreign competitors of Japanese manufacturers. Cultural and economic impediments to the use of JIT concepts outside Japan do not seem serious, as is being demonstrated by some of the Japanese subsidiary companies located in North America. Let us take a closer look first at JIT and then at total quality control blended with just-in-time. Marketing implications and the transportability of JIT/TQC are examined in the final sections of the chapter.

The Just-in-Time Concept

The just-in-time concept appears to be at the core of Japanese production management and productivity improvement. The JIT idea is simple: Produce and deliver finished goods just in time to be sold, subassemblies just in time to be assembled into finished goods, fabricated parts just in time to go into subassemblies, and purchased materials just in time to be transformed into fabricated parts. As one wag has put it, Japanese industry produces small quantities "just in time"; Western industry produces massive quantities "just in case." Like perfect quality, absolute just-in-time performance is never attained, but rather is an ideal to be pursued aggressively.

The JIT ideal is for all materials to be in active use as elements of work in process, never at rest collecting carrying charges. It is a hand-to-mouth mode of operation, with production and delivery quantities approaching one single unit—piece-by-piece production and material movement. At a Kawasaki Motors subsidiary plant in Lincoln, Nebraska, that ideal serves as a target, a dominant objective for the entire plant to shoot at year after year. Each move, anywhere in the plant, toward smaller production/delivery sizes achieves some of the promised JIT benefits.

Among the people who have attempted to explain JIT in English (a small number of writers), the prevailing view of JIT is as an inventory control system. In fact it is not uncommon to

16

Where the Words Came From

While *kanban* is a thoroughly Japanese word (meaning "card," or more literally, "visible record"), *just-in-time* is simply an English phrase that Japanese industry has adopted and that may not have a suitable Japanese equivalent. (Everyday conversation by Japanese business people is sprinkled with many such English words, especially technical terms.) It is hard to say when the term and the concept became important in Japanese industry. Some Japanese old-timers have told me that just-in-time came into wide use in the shipbuilding industry over 20 years ago. The story is that steelmakers had overexpanded; they had so much excess capacity that shipbuilders could get very fast deliveries on steel orders. The shipbuilders took full advantage of the situation, dropping their steel inventories from around one month's supply to a supply of perhaps three days. The shipbuilders were receiving their steel "just in time." The JIT (my abbreviation) idea spread to other Japanese OEM (original-equipment manufacturer) companies, who began demanding just-in-time deliveries from their suppliers —and began using JIT for internal operations as well. The world now knows about just-in-time, because since the mid-1970s Mr. Taiichi Ohno, a Toyota vice president, and several of Mr. Ohno's colleagues have been articulately explaining the concept in a series of articles, papers, and books. (The books are not available in English.) But, according to my sources, just-in-time was well under way in many Japanese companies before the writings appeared. This is not to deprecate Toyota's contribution, because the Toyota JIT system appears to be more advanced and to include more innovative features than that of any other Japanese company.

---

find just-in-time used synonymously with *kanban,* which is the name for a specific Japanese inventory replenishment system developed by Toyota. *Stockless production* is another term that is sometimes used. Kanban is indeed one device for moving toward JIT production, and "stockless production" captures the inventory control flavor of JIT. But I view just-in-time production management as much more. In upcoming chapters we will examine JIT as an inventory control system, as a quality and scrap control tool, as a streamlined plant configuration that raises process yield, as a production line balancing approach, and as an employee involvement and motivational mechanism. We will consider JIT applications starting with purchasing, proceding through manufacturing, and going all the way to distribution. But first, in the remainder of this chapter, we will take a closer look at the JIT process: (1) how lot-size reduction puts JIT into motion, (2) the chain reaction of benefits triggered by lot-size reduction, and (3) the blending of total quality control (TQC) with JIT.

Cutting Lot Sizes

It should be obvious that when you order in larger lots, the average inventory is larger, and you pay more inventory carrying charges. (Carrying charges are the interest costs on capital tied up in inventory, plus the physical holding costs, such as warehouse rent and warehouse workers' wages.) Therefore, if you want to cut carrying costs, just order smaller quantities more often.

But more frequent ordering has its costs, too. In factories, every time you reorder a component part, there is a setup cost. Setting up the equipment to run a particular component part often involves moving heavy dies into place and making numerous adjustments. Then a trial piece is run off, and an inspector checks it. The "first-piece inspection" often reveals a defect. More adjustments. Sometimes it takes hours before the settings seem right and production proceeds.

The labor involved in setup, plus scrapped parts and overhead costs, can push the setup cost to $50 or $500—or more. The manufacturing superintendent wants to hold down setup costs by setting up less often and making parts in larger quantities. A classic conflict shapes up: Finance wants to hold down carrying costs by small, frequent runs; manufacturing wants to hold down setup costs—and avoid production stoppages—by long, infrequent runs.

The resolution of the conflict is a pragmatic compromise.

18

There is an economically correct lot size—not so big as to incur an excessive carrying cost, not so small as to incur an excessive setup cost. The compromise quantity is known as the *economic order quantity* (EOQ), or economic lot size or run size. Figure 2–1 graphically shows how the EOQ is derived: The upward-slanting carrying cost line reflects the rising cost of larger lots; the downward-curving setup cost line reflects the falling cost of making parts less often (in larger lots). The sum of the two costs is the total cost curve, which bottoms out at the economically correct lot size, the EOQ.

The EOQ formula dates back to about 1915, when it was independently derived by Ford Harris and by R. H. Wilson. For years the EOQ has been a cornerstone of inventory management. It is time, however, to discard some of our EOQ training. The Japanese provide two reasons why:

1. Carrying cost and setup cost are only the obvious costs. Quality, scrap, worker motivation and responsibility, and manufacturing productivity are also significantly affected by manufacturing lot sizes. We shall study these effects later in the chapter.

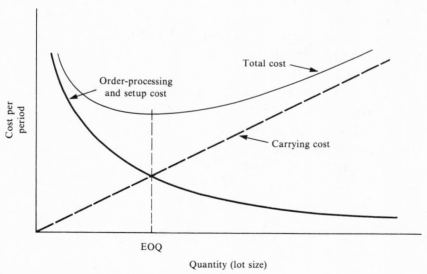

Figure 2–1. Economic Order Quantity

2. Setup cost is real and significant, but not unalterable. We are stuck with most carrying costs, but with ingenuity and resolve, setup costs can be driven down. Hall puts it this way:

> When the Japanese explain in detail how they achieved their big increases in productivity, the biggest "war stories" from the plant floor involve hard-fought battles to reduce setup times on a piece of equipment which at first was regarded as an insurmountable obstacle. Accounts of these battles detail changing the design of bolts, and the fit of pieces together on the machine. They describe the building of special tools to speed changeover, and practice sessions to learn how to perform changeovers quickly.[1]

Cutting Setup Times

One example of Japanese persistence in attacking setup problems is cited by representatives of Toyota's production control department.[2] A Toyota campaign to cut setup times began in 1971. In that year it took an hour to set up 800-ton presses used in forming auto hoods and fenders. After about five years of intensive engineering work, the setup time was down to 12 minutes. This compares, according to the authors, with six hours for a U.S. competitor; and Toyota was running lot sizes of just one day's worth of output per setup versus a reported 10 days' worth for the U.S. competitor.

But the 12-minute setup time is still too long. Toyota strives for "single setup," which means single-digit, i.e., less than 10 minutes. Toyota has often been able to reduce setup time to less than one minute, which is called "one-touch setup."[3] The two terms, single setup and one-touch setup, are now used in many Japanese companies, not just Toyota.

How is it possible to setup giant machine tools in under 10 minutes, or even in seconds? Hall provides further information about Toyota's hood and fender press operation:

> The press was modified to allow the old dies to quickly slide out of the press onto a waiting table while new dies are

20

pushed in from the other side. The workers performing the changeover "dry ran" the procedure so that it worked like kicking the extra point after a touchdown in football.[4]

Altering commercial machine tools for quick setup is widely practiced in Japanese industry. But the Japanese do not stop there. In many cases the solution to the setup time problem is to retire the commercial machine and to have the company's own toolmakers build their own machines. Self-developed machines and tools may be special-purpose, lightweight, easily moveable, and low-cost. Furthermore, setup time may be cut essentially to zero! That is, all the worker need do is load and unload; since the machine is designed for just one job, all dies, fixtures, and so forth may be built in so that there are no settings or adjustments. And it is not just the larger companies with fine toolmakers who make their own machine tools. I ran across a report by a delegation to Japan from Taiwan which noted that "even in small-scale Japanese industries, self-developed machines and tools were being used."[5] In a later chapter there is further discussion of self-developed tools, including examples.

Machine setup costs are such an obvious limitation to cutting inventories that one may wonder why only the Japanese have been worrying much about them. Some possible reasons are:

1. Our companies often have a variety of different brands of a given type of machine, bought, on the basis of low bids, from several different machine-tool manufacturers. With mixtures of equipment brands, developing setup-time-saving modifications is more costly. Because of luck or foresight, Kawasaki, Lincoln, found itself with nothing but Bliss punch presses when it embarked upon a campaign to cut setup times. Conversion of the Bliss presses, described in more detail later, was an early notable success in Kawasaki's program to implement just-in-time at its U.S. subsidiary plant.

2. There may be an attitude that you shouldn't tamper much with machine tools designed by experts like Warner and Swasey, Cincinnati Milicron, and Bliss; they are proven products, and

21

what is more, the resale value of such general-purpose equipment could be compromised if it is modified for your special jobs.

3. There may be a tendency for our upper managers, who generally have not come up through engineering and manufacturing, to scrutinize large obvious costs, like direct labor, tolerate a certain specified level of scrap and rework, and neglect setup cost and the like. Setup is the forgotten stepchild, treated as a given; scrap and rework are more like natural children: seen but not heard.

4. As I repeatedly state, we have not been aware of the chain reaction of benefits set in motion by cutting lot sizes; therefore, there has been inadequate Western motiviation to cut setup times. Kawasaki, Lincoln's full-scale campaign to adopt Japanese manufacturing management approaches began relatively recently—in about mid-1979. One reason why the program has gotten off the ground in so short a time is that Dennis Butt, an American who was plant manager at the time, had a good deal of prior manufacturing and engineering experience. He understood setup engineering—and readily grasped why the Kawasaki plants in Japan were so bent on engineering out the setup delays. Butt developed a set of graphs showing how the EOQ may be pushed downward—toward one unit—by cutting setup time and cost (see Figure 2–2). The rationale behind those graphs was drilled into the heads of Butt's staff of young American managers. (Some readers may have had occasion to see Butt's graphs inasmuch as Butt and some of his managers were invited speakers at several productivity and manufacturing management conferences around the United States.)

Cutting Purchase Order Costs

The economic order quantity concept is often used to determine purchase quantities as well as manufacturing lot sizes. The graph in Figure 2–1 may be applied to purchasing simply by considering

22

Figure 2–2. Economic Order Quantity Driven Down by Setup Time and Cost Reductions

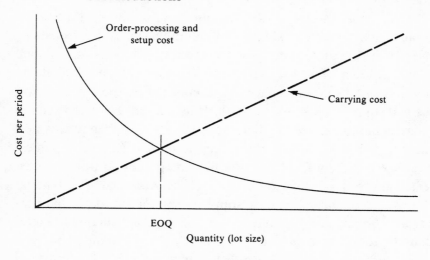

PRODUCTION IN LOTS

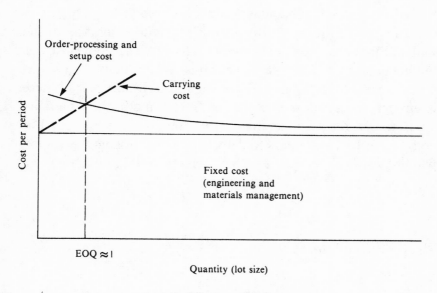

"LOTLESS" PRODUCTION

23

the downward-sloping cost line as representing purchase order cost, rather than setup cost.

The Japanese have attacked purchase order costs with the same zeal as setup costs. One way to cut purchase order costs is by simplifying the buying process. American buyers have a bag of well-known tricks for cutting purchasing red tape: blanket orders, stockless purchasing, vendor contracting, petty cash, approved supplier lists, and so forth. But U.S. buyers—and sellers—are generally shocked when they hear about how much farther the Japanese go in cutting purchasing activities. Buyer companies exercise close control over supplier companies so that there is less need for many of the usual American purchasing activities. For example, many Japanese suppliers routinely make deliveries of parts one or more times a day to the large original-equipment manufacturers, and the delivery quantity may be slightly changed daily based on just a phone call. Western suppliers, by contrast, typically deliver in full rail-car or truckload lots with a frequency more like once a month than every day; and formal paperwork—purchase orders, packing lists, bills of lading, invoices, and so forth—precedes, accompanies, and follows each delivery.

Several of the Japanese subsidiary plants operating in the United States have been endeavoring to introduce Japanese JIT buying practices into this country.[6] It is quite difficult to get U.S. suppliers to adapt, but there have been notable successes. There is enough to say on the subject of JIT buying in the American environment for a whole chapter, Chapter 7, in this book. But convincing U.S. suppliers to deliver just in time begins with explaining to them the far-reaching benefits of JIT, which will be discussed next.

The JIT Cause-Effect Chain

Japanese manufacturing management has caught the fancy of Western industry. Hundreds, perhaps thousands, of North

American plants have inaugurated some sort of program to try to catch up with the Japanese. Most programs are motivational: Organize Japanese-style employee participation groups, generally called quality circles. Other programs focus on plant modernization, including robotization. Still others feature tighter process controls on quality. More recently the word about just-in-time has gotten out, and plants are looking for ways to cut setup times, production lot sizes, and supplier delivery quantities.

The latter approach is especially attractive in that cutting lot sizes triggers a chain reaction of benefits—including motivational, quality, and plant improvement benefits. The chain of JIT effects is shown graphically in Figure 2–3. Lot-size reductions, shown in the double-bordered rectangle, set the chain in motion. The initial direct benefit is less inventory to carry and control (labled *A* in the figure). Probably more significant are the scrap and quality improvements that are likely to occur when lot sizes are reduced.

Scrap/Quality Improvements

The reason why minimum lot sizes lead to lower scrap and better quality may be simply explained: If a worker makes only one of a given part and passes it to the next worker immediately, the first worker will hear about it soon if the part does not fit at one of the next work stations. Thus, defects are discovered quickly and their causes may be nipped in the bud; production of large lots high in defects is avoided.

Scrap/quality improvement effects (labeled *B* in Figure 2–3) are maximal when lot sizes drop all the way to one-piece-at-a-time production. But any lot-size cuts at all should help. If you have been stamping out two days' worth—say, 2,000 units—of a certain bracket and now go to one day's worth, or 1,000, your level of quality awareness is sure to improve. You will be running the bracket job twice as often and will hear twice as soon about

25

Figure 2–3. Effects of JIT Production

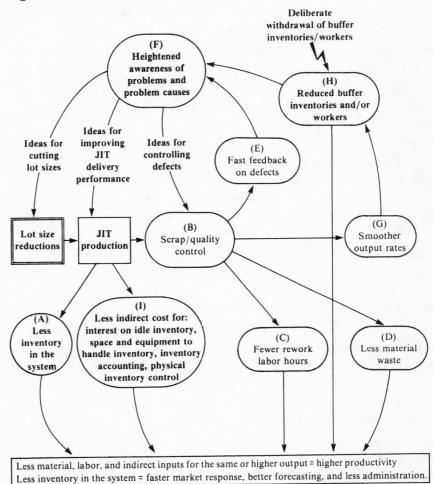

Less material, labor, and indirect inputs for the same or higher output = higher productivity
Less inventory in the system = faster market response, better forecasting, and less administration.

any defective brackets that you make. Your operation becomes more closely linked to the next process—say, a subassembly in which your bracket goes into a widget—and all following processes as well. The widget assembler may begin to see you and your stamping machine as the source of more brackets, whereas the source probably had previously seemed to be the lot-size inventory of brackets—before the lot-size pile was cut from two days' worth to one day's worth. You are aware of the widget assembler's new feeling of dependence upon your steady output of good brackets. You have reason to do better work. And you do.

The end result is, the customer is going to get better-quality goods. What is more, they will cost less. When JIT leads to reduced scrap and more good parts, the time and money spent on rework drops (labeled C in Figure 2–3), and so does the cost of wasted materials (labled D in the figure). As the quality control folks put it, "Quality is value added; all the rest is waste." But the benefits of better employee motivation may be just as significant.

Motivational Effects

We may expect (following psychologist B. F. Skinner's principles of reinforcement) that the worker who quickly learns the effects of his workmanship will become naturally motivated to improve. When JIT is in operation, there is no particular need for supervisors steeped in behavior-modification lore to provide pats on the back. The consequences of the worker's workmanship are visible quickly (labeled E in Figure 2–3) and are their own reward—or penalty.

But even if the principles of fast reinforcement were inoperative, the JIT mode would be likely to make the worker more conscientious. Under JIT, if a part doesn't fit at the next work station, the worker who made the bad part will probably not find it hard to guess what he did wrong. In short, the worker's awareness of defect causation is heightened (labeled F in Figure 2–3). To borrow a metaphor, under Western large-lot production, the large-lot-size inventories obscure problems much like high seas cover up dangerous rocks for the boatman. When the lot-size inventory is cut (the tide goes out), the causes of error (dangerous rocks) are exposed. Workers don't want to make bad parts any more than boatmen want to go aground on the rocks. Provide visiblity and each will steer a truer course.[7]

More specifically, there seem to be three kinds of positive response triggered by heightened awareness of problems and their causes. The workers and their bosses and staff advisers may generate:

- Ideas for controlling defects, which are fed back to further improve scrap/quality control.

- Ideas for improving JIT delivery performance (e.g., more convenient placement of parts to minimize handling delays), which are fed back to further streamline JIT production.

- Ideas for cutting setup time, which are fed back to further reduce lot sizes.

These three responses are shown by the three arrows leaving F in Figure 2–3. Each good idea for improvement ripples through the JIT cause-effect chain once more. Improvements feed upon improvements.

Responsibility Effects

A further deficiency of the large lot size is that it can provide convenient rationalization for carelessness on the part of the worker, the worker's peer group, and perhaps the labor union and management as well. They may feel, with some justification, that a certain percentage of bad parts in a large lot causes little harm; in a large lot there may be plenty of good items for every bad one. Just toss the defective aside and keep on assembling. With small JIT lot sizes, by contrast, a few defective parts pinch right away. The need to avoid errors is apparent, which improves workers' feelings of responsibility.

Western observers have marveled at how Japanese workers come to one another's aid to resolve problems. We might expect such behavior in a JIT plant, because with small-lot-size inventories, one worker's problem threatens to bring subsequent processes to a halt. All the workers—and their foremen—have production quotas to meet; withheld praise, enforced overtime, or reprimands are in store for those who fail to meet quotas. So it is natural for each affected worker to want to come to the aid of the worker whose drive belt breaks, whose machine is jammed, or who is having any of a large variety of other common problems.

Furthermore, Japanese labor unions have generally resisted bargaining for restrictive work rules that disallow the movement of workers from assigned stations, assigned trades, and assigned jobs to others. By contrast, Western workers protect their turf. Why? Why not? In Western plants brimming with inventory, the reason management would like to move a worker to another machine is often not to make a desperately needed part but rather to keep the worker or an expensive machine busy. The Japanese worker is told—or sees for himself—that he must be mobile in order to avoid parts stockouts, which might idle his buddies and bring on the consequences of quotas unmet.

It seems that there may not be a need to look for cultural explanations of the high levels of commitment that are apparent in Japanese workers. Their efforts are not buried in inventory as ours tend to be, so there is fertile ground for growth in feelings of responsiblity and commitment.

Small Group Improvement Activities

One thing leads to another. Committed workers carry their concerns—about defects, bottlenecks, slowdowns, breakdowns, and so forth—home with them, or to bars, bowling alleys, or other sites where they meet fellow workers. Shoptalk not only enters the conversations, but some employee peer groups in Japan even go so far as to organize themselves into so-called *small group improvement activities* (SGIAs), which is Toyota's name for what are also known as *quality control circles* (or quality circles).

The general impression in the United States is that the quality circle concept was a brilliant idea of Japanese management. Many quality circle proponents in this country believe that Japanese managers are well schooled in U.S. management writings on the values of employee participation and that quality circles were molded from employee participation principles. I offer an alternate explanation, discussed above: JIT lot-size inventory cuts raise worker commitment, which sometimes results in workers starting quality circle-like groups on their own initiative. And in Japan the need to conserve scarce material resources provided a favorable climate for the introduction of JIT in the first place. I do not mean to downplay the effectiveness of Japanese industrial managers, nor the difficulties in gaining the acceptance of JIT by the work force. Indeed, I believe that Japanese managers are remarkably effective. But part of the success formula was to capitalize upon simple, natural processes and human tendencies, such as those stemming from Japan's national needs to avoid waste. (Another ingredient in effective Japanese industrial management is the rather recent translation of those processes and tendencies into a production system with self-improving features, i.e., the just-in-time system with total quality control.)

When SGIAs or quality circles are in existence, these groups generate the three kinds of improvement ideas shown by the feedback arrows in Figure 2–3. But in a large-scale study a Harvard team did not find any Japanese subsidiaries in the United States using quality circles.[8] This might shock the legions of QC proponents here, as well as the many American companies that have established quality circle and SGIA programs.

Withdrawal of Buffer Inventory

What has been said so far about the JIT cause-effect chain does not require much day-to-day management intervention. The Japanese run a hand-to-mouth production system, with consequent high productivity, because they need to do so in order to conserve scarce resources. The Japanese are no longer the only nation faced with high costs to acquire and carry materials; perhaps the rest of the world now has its own reason for the JIT brand of belt tightening.

But there's more to the JIT story. The full just-in-time approach requires effective management to implement key system features, as well as daily managerial attention to make the system work. Japanese production management *system* innovations in just the last few years may help to explain why the results of Japanese productivity seem recently to have bombarded the West like a second wave of bombers applying the knockout punch in an airborne invasion. Toyota's manual *kanban* system and Yamaha's computer-based *synchro-MRP* system are among the hottest current topics at professional development meetings for various societies of production and inventory managers. (This began in about 1980 and was going strong by 1981. For example, in September 1981 I spoke to an audience of about 1,200 who packed the Grand Ballroom of the Sheraton Boston to hear about kanban and JIT.)

Another of the Japanese innovations involves turning a cherished old principle of inventory planning somewhat topsy-turvy. The principle has to do with buffer inventories, sometimes called safety stocks. So far our attention has been on lot-size inventories, whose sole reason for existence is the setup cost of making the lot (or the purchase order cost of buying it); if setup time and cost are zero, then the economic order quantity, or lot size, drops to one unit, which is the prerequisite for the JIT ideal: piece-for-piece processing. But even when the lot-size inventory is eliminated, there still is often a buffer inventory; the buffer stock is inserted between stations to cushion the shock of irregularities in the parts-feeder processes. The buffer inventory principle is, simply: The more irregularity, the more buffer stock. (There are statistical formulas for measuring the irregularities and mathematically translating the measurement into recommended buffer stock size.)

The Japanese no longer accept the buffer principle. Instead of adding buffer stocks at the points of irregularity, Japanese production managers deliberately expose the work force to the consequences. The response is that workers and foremen rally to root out the causes of irregularity. To ignore it is to face the consequences of work stoppages.

The Japanese principle of exposing the workers to the consequences of production irregularities is not applied passively. In the Toyota kanban system, for example, each time that workers succeed in correcting the causes of recent irregularity (machine jamming, cantankerous holding devices, etc.), the managers *remove still more buffer stock.* The workers are never allowed to settle into a comfortable pattern; or rather, the pattern becomes one of continually perfecting the production process. Toyota's small group improvement activities (SGIAs) never run out of new challenges. Whether the cycle of improvement can be sustained indefinitely remains to be seen.

The portion of Figure 2–3 affected by deliberate removal of buffer stock is highlighted in Figure 2–4. We see this managerial intervention in the shape of a lightening bolt. And indeed it is.

The removal of buffer stock, applied at point *H* in Figure 2–4, directly reduces inventory, which is productivity-enhancing (the same or more output with less material in the system). More importantly, the reduced buffer stock sets most of the JIT causal chain into motion. There is heightened awareness of the causes of irregular output (labeled *F* in Figure 2–4), which stimulates ideas for improvement. The JIT effects lead to smoother output rates—less irregularity (*G* in Figure 2–4)—which reduces the *need* for buffer stocks.

Figure 2–4. Effects of JIT Production

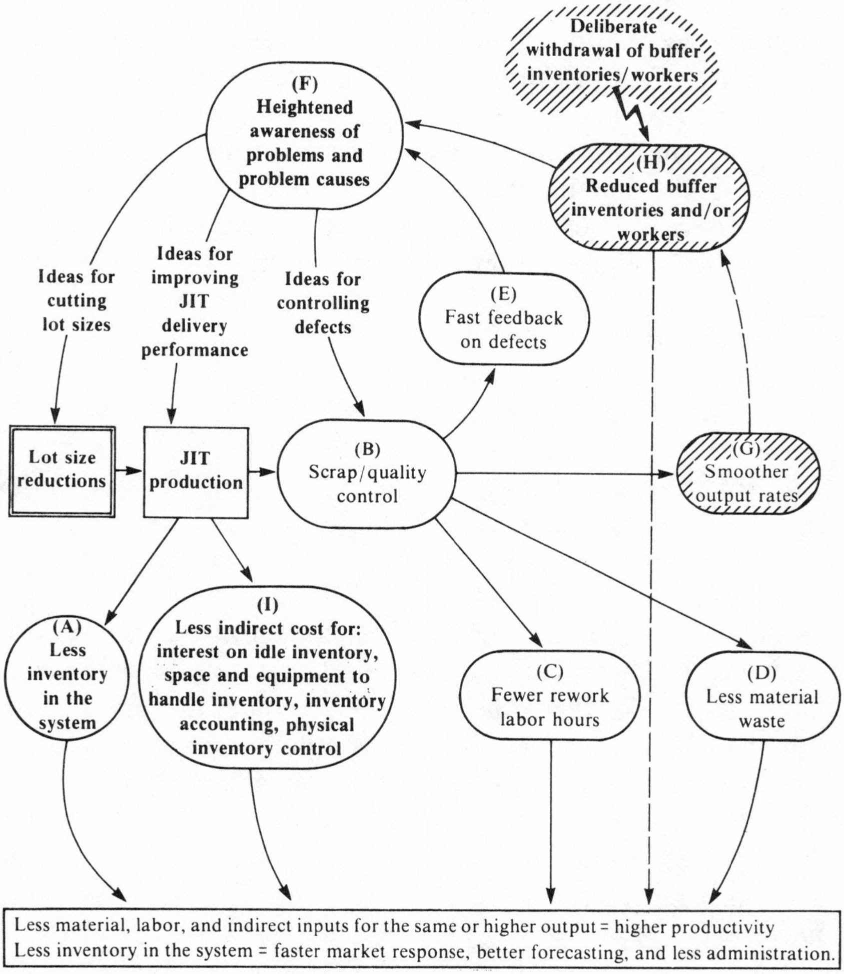

Indirect Labor Reductions

JIT inventory control yields indirect benefits (labeled *I* in Figure 2–4) as well as directly affecting workers and worker output. With less inventory there is less cost of interest on capital tied up in inventory. Also, there are fewer and smaller storerooms, much less space on the factory floor for work-in-process inventory, less inventory accounting, and less physical inventory control. Western industry features large materials-management staffs, numerous controlled-access storerooms, shop floors loaded with inventory, and dozens of materials-control forms and computer-output reports and files. By contrast, the Japanese prefer dock-to-line movement of materials received from suppliers, and lot-less, bufferless production and material movement within the plant.

Productivity and Market Response

The rectangle at the bottom of Figure 2–4 is a collector of all the JIT productivity enhancements—less lot-size inventory, less buffer inventory, less scrap, less direct labor wasted on rework, fewer indirect costs for interest on idle inventories, less space needed to store inventories, less equipment needed to handle them, less inventory accounting, and less physical inventory control—all of which lower the input component of the productivity equation. At the same time, the output component will be improved, since sources of delays and scrap are removed. Also, labor is more willing to move to where the work is and thereby stay productive, as opposed to Western labor's frequent insistence upon fixed work assignments (restrictive work rules).

A happy ancillary benefit of JIT is faster market response, better forecasting, and less administration. Less idle inventory in the system cuts overall lead time—from raw materials purchasing to shipping of finished goods. Marketing can thereby promise deliveries faster, can effect a change in the product mix or quantity faster, and can forecast demand better since the forecast horizon is not so far into the future. Inasmuch as JIT systems tend to be run by workers and foremen, the administrative budget

—for data processing, accounting, inspection, materials, control, production planning, and so forth—may be lean. Even executives are affected: With fire-fighting responsibilities clearly recognized and accepted by line workers, the executives may sit back and plan strategy. Indeed, all reports are that Japanese executives do just that.

The Total Quality Control Concept

Total quality control (TQC) may stand alone—or may operate in concert with just-in-time production. In the latter case, TQC greatly enhances the quality control aspects of the JIT model in Figures 2–3 and 2–4. Particularly affected are factors *B,C, D, E,* and *F* in the model; these are shaded in a new version of the JIT model shown in Figure 2–5.

In TQC, all plant personnel are inculcated with the view that quality control, factor *B* in Figure 2–5, is an end in itself. "Quality at the source" is the slogan that best epitomizes the TQC concept. What it means to the people in the plant is that errors, if any, should be caught and corrected at the source, i.e., where the work is performed. This is in contrast to the widespread Western practice of inspection by statistical sampling *after* the lot has already been produced: defect detection as opposed to defect prevention. In the Western system, the inspection is performed by inspectors from a quality control department; in Japanese TQC, workers and foremen (not a quality control department) have primary responsibility for quality, and everyone else is expected to contribute, often at the request of the workers and foremen: Engineers build automatic error-checking devices (aside from those supplied by equipment suppliers), personnel provides quality control training, management is quick to approve funding for any ideas that might enhance quality, and so forth.

35

Figure 2–5. Total Quality Control Blended with Just-in-Time Production

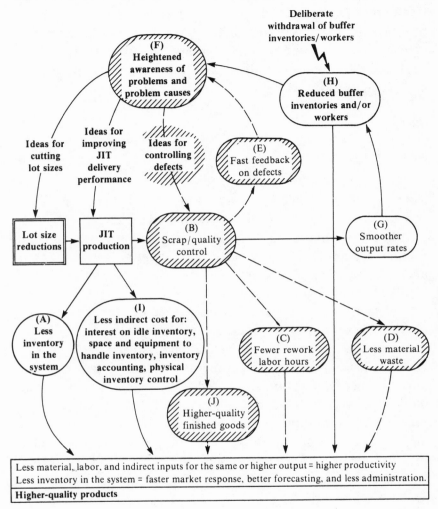

Less material, labor, and indirect inputs for the same or higher output = higher productivity
Less inventory in the system = faster market response, better forecasting, and less administration.

Higher-quality products

With quality control at the source, "fast feedback on defects," factor *E* in Figure 2–5, is natural. That is, it is the job of the worker (or of automatic checking equipment) to immediately check the quality of the part produced. Thus, the worker learns right away if a part is bad, which leads to "heightened awareness of problems and problem causes," factor *F* in Figure 2–5. Ideas for controlling defects are generated by the worker, the work group, the foreman, and various engineers or others who might be called in to help. New controls on defects further enhance scrap/quality control (factor *B*), and the cycle repeats—and blends in with the JIT cycle of cutting lot sizes and streamlining production.

The effects of TQC are "fewer rework labor hours" and "less material waste," factors *C* and *D* in Figure 2–5. In addition, there is "higher quality of finished goods," a new factor, *J*, in the figure. In the earlier discussion of the JIT concept, higher quality of finished goods was not claimed as an effect of JIT, because (a devil's advocate might argue) equally high product quality *could* be attained in a Western plant by means of extensive final inspection plus rework lines and scrap bins. That is, JIT will *not necessarily* improve product quality (but it will certainly lower costs). Total quality control, by contrast, certainly will improve product quality.

The Japanese attack on bad quality, now over 30 years old, has led to widespread Japanese use of a number of quality control procedures. These range from zealous maintenance of plant cleanliness, to use of statistics and fishbone charts showing causes and effects, to quality control circles, to workers' authority to halt production lines to correct a quality problem. These and other procedures will be examined in more detail in a later chapter.

Strategy: Market Dominance

It is easy to see that just-in-time production with total quality control can be an important cog in a Japanese manufacturer's strategy of international market dominance. (The success of that strategy—in cameras, consumer electronics, autos, watches, shipbuilding, and so forth—is well known and need not be rehashed here.) The never-ending JIT cycle of inventory cuts, quality and productivity improvements, more cuts, more improvements, and so on, results in ever-cheaper, ever-better goods—and total quality control greatly stimulates the rate of quality improvement. The competition can only be bewildered and demoralized by the resulting low-cost, high-quality Japanese products.

As if that weren't enough, the Japanese employ marketing and pricing tactics that, in effect, cause the JIT/TQC cycle to speed up. These tactics are aimed at getting initial sales contracts, which increases demand and required production volume. In various ways, higher volume smooths out some of the kinks in a JIT/TQC system. These points warrant some elaboration.

Marketing and Pricing

A Japanese marketing tactic that has been closely examined in the Western press is the practice of selling through giant Japanese trading companies specializing in export marketing. The trading companies take over the burdensome job of dealing with many countries in regard to foreign exchange, tariffs, quotas, shipping, administrative red tape, political considerations, and local customs. Each trading company will sell products for a wide diversity of Japanese producers. The typical fee of 30 percent is high but can be quite worthwhile for providing for entry to export markets.

A Japanese pricing tactic is simply to accept small profit margins. This practice has also been examined in the Western press, usually in connection with reflections on the Japanese long-run outlook as compared with the West's obsessive need to meet short-term profit targets: the Western company tends to avoid or drop products with modest profit margins, partly because of the personal risks of not meeting next quarter's or next year's profit target. The Japanese don't do this. According to popular thinking, the reasons are that the Japanese have a longer-term outlook. Apparently Japanese managers are thought to be more patient or more insightful, or perhaps less greedy. I haven't run across any explanations of how they got that way. But never mind; more logical explanations than "a longer-term outlook" are available.

Good explanations for accepting a low profit margin are:

1. Lower quoted prices help get *initial* sales contracts (which complement the efforts of the trading companies).

2. *Keeping* the profit margin low adds more contracts, which increases total demand and required production volume —which helps to accelerate productivity improvement, especially if the Japanese producer has a JIT/TQC system. As productivity improves with higher volume, unit cost drops and quality improves so that the selling price can be further cut, thus capturing a still greater market share. The profit margin can stay low, but overall profitability will be high because of large sales volume.

Cost-Volume Relationship

Western industry is quite aware of these phenomena. The well-known learning curve (or experience curve) concept captures the idea of decreasing unit cost with increasing volume. The Boston Consulting Group has gotten a good deal of mileage out of the experience curve in its management consulting in recent years. A number of Western companies—Texas Instruments is the most publicized example—have been able to capture considerable market share by means of experience curve pricing.

Leading Japanese manufacturers tend to place even more faith in this cost-volume relationship. One version of the relationship that seems to be particularly popular in Japan is the pseudo-

39

mathematical expression $2V = 2/3\ C$, where V = volume of productive output and C = cost per unit. The expression is not intended for mathematical purposes, but rather is interpreted intuitively to mean: Doubling the volume results in two-thirds of the unit cost.[9] This expression reflects a 67 percent (2/3) learning curve, which actually means 33 percent learning, or cost reduction, for each doubling of volume. Thirty-three percent is a very high rate of learning; 5 to 20 percent is more typical for Western firms using the learning curve. A difference is: The typical Western attitude is that learning occurs of its own accord—typically at a 5 to 15 percent rate; the Japanese, by contrast, are improvement-oriented. That is, they strive to make learning/productivity/cost reduction happen. The advanced state-of-the-art mechanism for making it happen is the just-in-time production system.

The Partnership of Marketing and JIT

The volume-cost relationship just discussed is well known in the West. The economies-of-scale idea has long been a fundamental concept in our economics courses. Furthermore, plenty of Western companies employ the somewhat risky strategy of small profit margins to stimulate market penetration.

The strategy is not so risky when coupled with a just-in-time production system and total quality control. As has been noted, higher volumes smooth out some of the wrinkles in the JIT/TQC system. It works like this:

A small manufacturer attempting to implement JIT/TQC must employ extensive engineering to cut setup times and thereby make small-lot production more economical, and to design automatic quality-checking devices and thereby improve control of quality at the source. Since the extensive engineering is expensive, the pace of moving toward JIT/TQC is slow. But if the company's volume doubles, the cost of each change may be amortized over twice as many units produced; the pace of setup-time reductions and installation of quality-checking devices thus increases.

Secondly, if the volume doubles, some processes that had been configured as general-purpose machine centers producing in lots may be reconfigured as multiple production lines, each dedicated to making a single component part in a piece-by-piece pure JIT mode with sophisticated quality controls. (Plant configurations for JIT production are explained in detail in Chapter 5.) Dedicated lines are not feasible unless the volume is large enough to keep the lines relatively busy.

Thirdly, high volume makes it attractive to cease running to a schedule and instead fabricate subassemblies and parts based on the *need* of a "downstream" stage of manufacture. This is the idea behind the kanban system of parts ordering, which is known as a *pull* system. That is, the using (downstream) stage "pulls" parts from the producing stage, as needed, through successive stages of manufacture. The pull system matches production with need. This results in less inventory than a schedule-based system, because a schedule is really a "guesstimate" of needs—a guesstimate that includes buffer inventory to protect against error. High volume also makes it possible to manufacture a fairly steady daily quantity of each major end product, which is a prerequisite for kanban.

In these ways and perhaps others, the movement toward a just-in-time/total-quality-control operation, with its attendant improvements in productivity, quality, and cost reduction, is speeded up. Sales and production increases are the facilitator, but without deliberate continual management effort to make JIT improvements, the improvements would be likely only to approximate the normal Western learning curve rate, i.e., 5 to 20 percent as the quantity doubles. To achieve a rate close to the 33 percent Japanese target requires active, not passive, response to the opportunities offered by volume growth.

In summary, a strategy of market dominance in top Japanese firms is likely to be viewed mainly as a *production* achievement, with marketing and pricing aggressiveness providing momentum to speed up the rate. By contrast, the production function is likely to be seen as a bystander in Western firms that have managed to capture market share.

Symbiosis

A popular buzzword in college classrooms is *symbiosis*. It means a successful pooling of efforts; a good fit. We have just seen how the JIT/TQC strategy is mutually advantageous for marketing and production, with competitive advantages for the firm as a whole. Earlier discussion showed how JIT-induced inventory reductions foster mutual dependency relationships, and how the TQC concept of quality at the source further increases awareness of interdependency—with the happy result that people pull together. A highly symbiotic work environment is created in which improvements—such as cutting inventory, staff, or defect causes—expose problems, which motivates further improvements. The message to Western companies, where inventories and other excesses have hidden the problems and squelched such symbiotic effects, may be expressed as follows: *Those who have had plenty for themselves and little need to share with others may learn to cooperate if that plenty is removed.*

Transportability

Culture does not travel well. Management systems, however, are quite transportable. I have tried to show that high Japanese productivity has been achieved through use of innovative manufacturing management and marketing approaches, which were spawned in the unique Japanese environment. Japanese industrial managers learned how to cope with high costs of materials, energy, and space by means of the simple but highly effective just-in-time and total quality control system. JIT/TQC development began rather naturally but recently has been infused with new management principles (e.g., attacking setup times, deliberate removal of buffer stock, and rejection of an "acceptable quality level") and systems (e.g., kanban and synchro-MRP). One has to be particularly impressed with the apparent wide understanding among Japanese industrial managers at all levels of the powerful effects of simple triggering mechanisms, such as setup cost reductions. The Japanese seem to be able to let the simple system work—and resist the Western impulse to turn productivity and quality improvement over to armies of staff specialists.

Since most Western manufacturers presently have such armies of staff specialists, what are the prospects for JIT/TQC program success in Western plants? The years will tell, but examination of JIT in action with U.S. workers provides some answers. Tentative conclusions can be drawn from the two-year-old JIT program at Kawasaki Motors in Lincoln, Nebraska (apparently the first and nearly the only plant in the United States with a full commitment to JIT), and from several cases of TQC in other Japanese plants in the United States. Kawasaki's JIT history, plus some JIT practices at TRI-CON, Sony, and Honda plants in the United States, form part of the basis for discussion of JIT in remaining chapters. Experiences in several Japanese electronics plants in this country—Sanyo in particular—are discussed in connection with total quality control. (There are not yet any good examples of Japanese subsidiaries that have fully developed both JIT and TQC in the same U.S. plant. The Japanese automotive companies that are getting started here—Honda in Ohio and Nissan in Tennessee—have competitive needs in both the productivity and quality areas, and are thus likely to aggressively pursue both JIT and TQC from the outset.) The overall conclusion is that JIT/TQC generally should work in the United States, though not in just the same way as in Japan.

43

Muri, Muda, Mura (むり, むだ, むら)

Some of the fundamentals of this chapter are nicely encompassed by the Japanese plea: Avoid *muri, muda, mura. Muri* means "excess," *muda* means "waste," and *mura* means "unevenness." The alliterative quality of the three words, as well as their symbolic brevity, has made them a popular expression among Japanese manufacturing people.[10] The expression provides a particularly appropriate note on which to end the chapter, inasmuch as the three words relate closely to three cherished principles of Western management that have been overturned by the Japanese experience with JIT/TQC:

1. *Muri.* The Western principle of ordering in economic order quantities (EOQ) is, in the Japanese just-in-time system, an example of *muri,* or excess. JIT calls for ordering in lots that are smaller than the EOQ, ideally just one unit, because:

> a. The EOQ formula fails to account for several benefits of smaller lot sizes, including scrap/quality improvement; less rework; and fast feedback on errors, which leads to problem awareness and solution.

> b. The EOQ formula takes setup/order cost as a given, but in the Japanese system setup/order cost is continually reduced.

2. *Muda.* The Western principle of statistical sampling of lots by quality control department inspectors presumes and allows for a certain percentage of defectives, which the Japanese view as *muda,* or waste. JIT/TQC prescribes:

> a. Elimination of lots altogether (ideally) so that there can be no lots to sample from and no chance of a certain percentage of defectives per lot.

b. Quality at the source featuring workers, not QC department inspectors, in charge of preventing defectives from occurring and then moving on, undetected, to subsequent processes.

3. *Mura*. The Western buffer stock principle, calling for inventory to protect one work center from the output variability of the preceding work center, is, in the JIT approach, irrational acceptance of *mura,* or unevenness. The JIT solution is to do exactly the opposite: *remove* buffer stock to *expose* the variability—and correct the underlying causes (instead of adding buffer stock to hide the problems).

Thus, the lesson of this chapter, in Japanese, is to avoid *muri, muda,* and *mura.* In English, the second lesson may be restated:

The just-in-time/total-quality-control system is an imperative to continually improve.

CHAPTER 3

Total Quality Control

LESSON 3: Quality begins with production, and requires a company-wide "habit of improvement."

> The theme . . . is "make them right the first time." Emphasis is on defect prevention so that routine inspection will not be needed to as large an extent. The burden of quality proof rests not with inspection but with the makers of the part: machinist, assembly foremen, vendor, as the case may be.

Does the above quotation sound familiar? Like something you read in a *Time* or *Fortune* article on Japanese management of quality? There have been a number of such explanations of Japanese quality in the press. But this quotation comes from a 1961 book by a respected U.S. quality control authority, A. V. Feigenbaum.[1] The theme is part of what Feigenbaum called "total quality control," and over the years in the United States many quality engineers learned about the approach through use of Feigenbaum's book, as a text or reference source. While the engineers often know about total quality control, U.S. management virtually never heard of it—until recently, when some of their touring delegations to Japan were told about it.

Unfortunately, many Westerners who hear about total quality control probably think that it refers to *quality control circles* or that it is about the same thing as *zero defects*. The zero defects (ZD) concept was initiated in the United States over 20 years ago, and a fair number of Western manufacturers have installed ZD programs. The popular ZD slogan "Quality is everybody's business" sounds as if it captures the flavor of "total quality control." As for the quality control circle, it is a formally constituted group of workers and supervisors who meet to talk about ways to improve quality or other aspects of the work environment. Getting workers involved in quality control circles, like ZD, has a "total quality" ring to it.

The truth is that QC circles and ZD programs are far too limited in scope to be represented as the Japanese formula for achieving exceptionally high quality levels. Furthermore, total quality control, as practiced in Japanese industry today, considerably extends and elaborates upon the 1961-vintage TQC proposed by Feigenbaum. Feigenbaum's message was fundamental. It took the Japanese to figure out a way to make worker-level process control work. This chapter will carefully examine how the Japanese "operationalized" total quality control. A later chapter will consider the role of quality control circles in the TQC movement, as well as related Western work improvement programs like zero defects.

Total Quality Control Concepts

Feigenbaum stated that "the burden of quality proof rests . . . with the makers of the part." It takes only a slight change in wording to translate that clause into the basic precept of Japanese TQC: The *responsibility for* quality rests with the makers of the part. ''Burden of proof'' has a defensive connotation; ''responsibility for'' fundamentally alters the quality formula by making quality control a basic production objective requiring *offensive* policies, strategies, and procedures.

In U.S. plants, the business of production is production. Efficiency reports and salaries are based on it. If you ask about quality in a U.S. plant, you are referred to the quality control department. If U.S. companies want to improve quality to match the Japanese, the first step must be to place responsibility for quality in the hands of the production department—and remove it from the quality control department.

Responsibility

This prescription for change is of a type that U.S. management is particularly adept at accomplishing: reorganizing and reassigning responsibility. When an American company reassigns a responsibility, an avalanche of standards, measures, and controls swiftly follows to assure that the inheritors of the responsibility perform it.

It really is not necessary to tell the manager with the responsibility *how* to perform it. If incentives—measures of performance and the like—are there, ways to achieve performance will be found. What I am emphasizing is that the mere act of reassigning responsibility for quality to the production department is likely to get some results in steadily improving quality.

Learning from the West

This is not to say that proper assignment of responsibility is enough—that quality control techniques are unimportant. An early stage in the transformation of Japanese industry from poor to excellent quality was intensive study of Western quality control techniques and concepts. The works of two Americans, Joseph M. Juran and W. Edwards Deming, are often cited by the Japanese as being highly influential. In the last 30 years or so, Juran and Deming have made repeated visits to Japan as lecturers and consultants. Other Western quality control textbooks and handbooks have also been important, especially Feigenbaum's *Total Quality Control,* a title that is also the term used to represent current Japanese practices (which go far beyond what was recommended in the book).

Juran, Deming, Feigenbaum, and others have, of course, been spreading the same messages in North America and Western Europe. The Japanese environment perhaps explains why the message "took" so much better there than in the West. The environmental factors I refer to are: (1) The age-old Japanese penchant for avoiding the waste of scarce resources, that is, the waste entailed in making bad goods; (2) a cultural climate in which the self-serving tendencies engendered by specialism, including specialism in quality control, do not fit in—which leads to leaving responsibility for quality in its natural place, the place where the production is performed.

TQC Concepts Categorized

Deming seems to be thought of as the father of Japanese quality control. A prize named after him, the annual Deming Prize, has been awarded for some 30 years to the Japanese manufacturer exhibiting the most impressive quality performance. There is enough nationwide interest that the awarding of the prize is now nationally televised.

Deming places great store in the use of statistics: statistical quality control and frequency distribution statistics on quality levels. The Japanese have massively trained people in industry in the use of these kinds of statistical tools, and they appear to be in wide use. However, I believe that the statistical tools are not quite so important in the spectrum of concepts that constitute Japanese total quality control as are some of the more conceptual factors. Figure 3–1 is my attempt to group the large number of TQC factors into categories, roughly arranged in order of importance to a Western manufacturer.

The first TQC category, organization, consists of the most essential concept, *production responsibility*. As has already been discussed, this means assigning the primary responsibility for quality to the production people—and removing it from the quality control department. This should be the first step for the Western company that is serious about quality improvement.

Beyond that, the *rate* of quality improvement can be accelerated a good deal by implementing items from TQC categories 2 through 5 in Figure 3–1. These categories include the TQC goals, basic principles, facilitating concepts, and techniques and aids

TQC CATEGORY	TQC CONCEPT
1. Organization	Production responsibility
2. Goals	Habit of improvement Perfection
3. Basic principles	Process control Easy-to-see quality Insistence on compliance Line stop Correcting one's own errors 100 percent check Project-by-project improvement
4. Facilitating concepts	QC as facilitator Small lot sizes Housekeeping Less-than-full-capacity scheduling Daily machine checking
5. Techniques and aids	Exposure of problems Foolproof devices N = 2 Analysis tools QC circles

Figure 3–1. Total Quality Control: Concepts and Categories

that have been tried out and molded to a high level of effectiveness in Japanese industry since about 1962. In that year, *Gemba To QC,* the Japanese quality control journal for foremen, began publication. The journal was written in plain, shop-oriented language and provided an effective way for quality control ideas that are feasible at the level of the work center to be shared.

The years of experience and improvement in Japanese industry yield a long list of quality concepts, which I have grouped into categories 2, 3, 4, and 5 in Figure 3–1. Many of the items listed have been successfully implemented with American middle managers and workers in some of the Japanese subsidiaries operating in the United States, especially in electronics, where quality is rather more essential than price.

TQC categories 2 to 5 in Figure 3–1 consist of some concepts that are in opposition to what we Westerners have believed in, some approaches that we never thought of, and some practices that are adaptations of Western ways. Some of the basic principles (category 3) are of the latter variety, while the goals, considered next, are in basic opposition to common Western practice.

Goals

The goals of total quality control (category 2 in Figure 3–1) are twofold and closely related. The operational goal is to sustain the habit of quality improvement, while the target is, simply, perfection. The operational goal pursues the target.

The Habit of Improvement

In the Western system, goals tend to be static—at least until the next fiscal year, when new goals may be established. The static goals serve as standards, and our managers' focus is on control, or minimizing variance from the standards. The Western habit of control encompasses the budget, use of materials, and various other factors including quality.

On the other hand, as Juran notes, "Over the years the accumulated experience [of the Japanese] has developed its own imperative—the precious *habit of improvement*."[2] Control keeps things stable, but while the Western company is maintaining stability, the Japanese company keeps improving.

Perfection

The habit of improvement is directed toward perfection. The goal of perfection is partly in agreement with and partly in contrast to what is preached in Western quality control books and practiced in most Western manufacturing companies. Here are some of the points of agreement and disagreement:

- *Agreement.* Quality performance, at any given time, is measured by how well the product conforms to design specifications.

- *Disagreement.* The short-run quality target in Western industry presumes a given percentage of defectives. The target in Japanese industry is to accept no historical defect rate but to press for perfect conformance to specifications.

- *Agreement.* Quality depends on the efforts of marketing, design engineering, purchasing, manufacturing engineering, production, quality control, packaging, shipping, and service departments.

- *Disagreement.* Western industry presumes that there is an optimum level of quality effort that should be exerted; customers' willingness to pay the costs of quality is the limiting factor. Japanese industry has adopted a quality

53

strategy which, without reckless disregard for costs of quality, presumes that ever-better quality will forever increase market share and the total market as well.

It is true that the term "zero defects," which sounds like "perfection," is a Yankee invention, spawned in the aerospace industry during the early days of the manned space program. And if you were to ask a manager in a Japanese company what its quality goal was, the likely reply would be "zero defects." The Japanese know all about our ZD programs; they like the expression and they use it.

The ZD notion is well known in the West as well, and quite a few Western companies give lip-service to the term. Also, a fair number of companies have a ZD program, in which workers are indoctrinated with the notion that a defect is not normal—that perfect conformity to design specifications is realistic and should be the goal. Western ZD programs rely largely on persuasion. The zero defects idea is persuasive enough that ZD programs frequently are beneficial—in spite of being forced to exist in the same old company settings geared for static, rather than improving, standards of quality. About the only organizational changes are appointment of a ZD program coordinator and ZD committee; the only change in techniques is to place "error-cause removal" forms in convenient locations so that workers can note obstacles in the way of their attainment of zero defects. By contrast, in the Japanese TQC system, with a goal of perfection, organizational responsibility for quality is entirely realigned, and a host of supporting principles, concepts, techniques, and aids are implemented to drive the organization toward the goal.

As was mentioned, the Japanese are more likely to use the term "zero defects" than "perfection." I have chosen to use the latter term, because perfection more nearly captures the Japanese marketing strategy of pressing onward for better and better quality in order to increase the market and their own company's share of it. ("Build a better mousetrap, and the world will beat a path to your door"—a proverb attributable to Ralph Waldo Emerson, an American, and widely practiced by the Japanese.)

Both terms, perfection and zero defects, have a somewhat silly, pie-in-the-sky ring to them. They are obviously not attainable. Still, the terms are appropriate, because they stick in people's consciousness (and are the stuff of nice slogans and banners) —as a goal, not as a claim.

Basics

Seven basic principles of total quality control are listed in Figure 3–1: process control, easy-to-see quality, insistence on compliance, line stop, correcting one's own errors, 100 percent check, and project-by-project improvement. The first two are closely related and equally important.

Process Control

Process control, the first principle, is a standard Western quality control concept. It means controlling the production process by checking the quality while the work is being done. The Western practice is to control certain processes by means of process control inspections during production, and our quality control books try to tell us how best to select the processes to be inspected. Beyond that, we rely on final inspections of completed lots (called lot-acceptance inspection). In Japanese TQC, the *T* stands for "total," and that means, above all, *total process control:* Every process is to be controlled by checking the quality during production. Of course, no Western company can afford total process control, because it does not have enough inspectors. It would seem that the quality control department would need about as many inspectors as there are production workers in order to inspect quality during every process. Having already discussed Japanese responsibility for quality being assigned to production rather than quality control departments, now we see a chief reason why: The only affordable way to control quality in all processes is for workers to do it themselves. Every work station may be an inspection point.

In Western quality control books, discussion of process control centers on statistical quality control (SQC) charts, developed by QC department specialists. Many Japanese foremen and workers have learned about SQC charts, but that is a lesser point to be considered later.

Easy-to-See Quality

Easy-to-see quality, the second principle, is an extension of an established Western principle of "measurable standards of quality." Deming and Juran emphasized this principle perhaps above all others in their lectures in Japan in the 1950s. So well have the Japanese learned this lesson that even the Boy Scout troop on a plant tour will see how quality is measured. Display boards are everywhere in Japanese plants. They tell the worker—and the bosses, and customers, and outside visitors—what quality factors are measured, what the recent performance is, what the current quality improvement projects are, who has won awards for quality, and so forth. Some displays are lighted electronic devices —resembling basketball scoreboards—which call for help when there are quality problems.

Clearly the Japanese place great stock in our notion of measurable standards of quality, but making those measures easy to see is purely a Japanese idea. It takes time and money to make process quality visible, and the Western observer may wonder— as I did initially—"Why bother?"

My own personal enlightenment began in a conference with Takashige Yamane, manager of quality control at Mitsuboshi

Belting Co. in Kobe, Japan. Mr. Yamane was telling me how inspection teams from customer plants (auto companies) will invite themselves to tour Mitsuboshi's plant (making auto V-belts and hoses) whenever they get sufficiently peeved. The inspection teams poke their noses into everything from quality control charts to equipment maintenance records to the food in the cafeteria, and they generally leave a list of as many as 200 demerits that they want corrected.

The inspectors particularly demand visual, obvious indicators of quality at every process (total process control), and the indicators must be easy to understand, e.g., not a page of computer listings understandable only to a technician. In effect, the customer teams are saying "You tell us that you have total quality control. But where's the evidence? We want to see and understand it for ourselves." The company that has not clearly and simply defined what good quality is—and the converse, what constitutes a defective—cannot make quality visual, and the customer may find a supplier who can. (Mitsuboshi does the same thing to its suppliers; for example, Mr. Yamane occasionally leads a team to inspect the plants of the suppliers of the fabric that lends strength to rubber V-belts.)

This practice has been going on long enough in Japan so that some plants seem almost to have been designed with the quality inspector in mind. One such plant is a Matsushita refrigerator factory at Lake Biwa in Japan. Wide aisles and pointed arrows direct the visitor through the plant. Improvements in methods and in quality—especially quality—are extolled on display signs in nearly every work area. The displays include plaques and other awards presented to groups or individuals, so that the visitor will see a picture of total work-force involvement in quality. I had seen much the same thing (except for the arrows and other directional aids obviously aimed at visitors) in *every* Japanese plant that I visited.

What I was not prepared for at Matsushita was testing equipment—carefully calibrated gauges, meters, and so forth—on display in work areas along the tour route. The equipment was contained (when not in use) in dustfree locked glass cases of the type that one sees in a jewelry store. Similarly, several quality testing rooms—gauge room, chemical lab, calorimeter room, test room, soundproof test room, "torture" room, etc.—were paneled in glass facing the visitors' tour route. The floor in the final assembly area, where trays and other components were manually stuffed into refrigerators, was hospital-clean.

Touring inspectors, perhaps a team of buyers from Takashimaya Department Store, are sure to be impressed that Matsushita not only says its refrigerators are good but can visually convince them by ostentatiously displaying everything conceivably related to quality in the factory. Still, the inspection party will find flaws and present its list of demerits. If welding defects are currently in the order of 50 parts per million (PPM), the inspectors may press for 40 PPM; their inspection will include the purchasing department, and a recommendation might be for Matsushita to reconsider company X as a source of better welding rods.

In contrast to Matsushita's new, highly automated "showcase" refrigerator plant, Mitsuboshi's rubber V-belt and hose factory in Kobe is ancient and worn. (Mitsuboshi has newer plants that I did not visit.) Still, the Mitsuboshi plant was proud to display its extensive dedication to improvement of quality. I am very familiar with a similarly ancient V-belt and hose factory operated by Goodyear in the United States. Goodyear is working hard to paint, fix up, modernize, and improve the productivity of the plant. (Goodyear people have toured Japanese plants, including Mitsuboshi, and they know what they are up against.) But Goodyear has no particular incentive to develop easy-to-see quality indicators, as Mitsuboshi does. It may take a few years, but the incentive will come. General Motors, Ford, and Chrysler know that Nissan and Toyota quality-inspect their suppliers' plants, and they are leaders among American companies in doing the same sort of thing.

Some U.S. companies have experienced the invasion of Japanese buyer representatives conducting thorough inspections of their plants. For example, Webco Lumber Co., a small California enterprise in danger of succumbing to the current recession, sent a team to Japan to drum up customers. Customers they got. Representatives from two dozen Japanese companies descended upon the California mill to see if the mill could meet their exacting quality standards. "They did everything from measuring the thickness of our saw to measuring the ring counts of our logs," recalls Barbara Webb, the president of Webco. "They're real tire-kickers," adds another Webco official. Webco got Japanese orders and is now one of the few thriving mills on the West Coast. But the pre-contract inspection was not the only Japanese visit. Webco's first Japanese customer sent a representative to monitor the cutting and planing. The Japanese man periodically halted the planing and cutting operations to check the lumber's dimensions, so that the order took about twice as long to complete as is normal.[3]

So, U.S. suppliers . . . Get ready. Your customers (e.g., Ford or Nissan, Zenith or Sony) will want to inspect your plant. They will *demand* measurable standards of quality at every process, and they will coax you toward simple, easy-to-see indicators of quality. And you should do the same with your suppliers.

Insistence on Compliance

The third principle, insistence on compliance, also has Western roots but has tended to be honored in the breach in much of Western industry. That is, a lax atmosphere exists in which QC department inspectors frequently give in to pressure from manufacturing to pass parts and subassemblies that actually do not quite meet established quality standards. It is not hard to change this state of affairs. Top management merely needs to inform manufacturing that quality comes first and output second, and insist on it. We see evidence of Western companies altering their priorities in just that way. For example, in a TV commercial for

Ford a production-line worker says, "All I know is that what was good last year—this year wouldn't make the grade."

Line Stop

The fourth basic principle, line stop, is closely related to the third. The Japanese *do* make quality the first priority and output second, and line stop—giving each worker the authority to stop the production line to correct quality problems—puts teeth in the priority policy. In more mechanized processes line stops may be automatically accomplished by checking devices attached to the equipment, which are further discussed under the heading "Foolproof Devices" later in the chapter. (The Japanese word *jidoka* refers to the overall concept that governs the line-stop principle.)

At Kawasaki's U.S. plant, assembly lines are strung with yellow and red lights; workers press the yellow when there is a problem and the red when the problem is serious enough for a line stop. Sometimes the line stops are necessitated by direct quality problems, such as parts not fitting quite right, and the problem needs to be noted and immediately forwarded to the work centers that made the poorly fitting parts. In nearly all cases the stop assures that the assemblers will take enough time to make sure that *they* are not the cause of bad quality.

By contrast, in Western plants, where output is the number one priority, the production process does not slow or stop for such things. The response to problems is simply to leave out bolts, omit certain weldments, miss spots with paint sprayers, and so forth. The workers cannot be blamed for such behaviors, nor can foremen. Management has not given them line-stop authority, so the output is steady but the quality is uneven.

Correcting One's Own Errors

The principles of process control, easy-to-see quality, insistence on compliance, and line stop help to enforce the assignment of responsibility for quality to the production department. The fifth basic principle, correcting one's own errors, closes the loop. Primarily, the principle refers to rework: The worker or work group that made the bad parts performs the rework itself to correct the errors.

This is a major departure from Western practice, in which separate rework lines with their own crews are usual. It *seems* efficient to perform rework in a separate area, because routing bad parts, subassemblies, or end products back through the main work areas can be a handling problem, which, in a Western plant, would disrupt the normal scheduled output rate.

In Japanese plants output *rate* is not important; as we have seen, the rate can be interrupted at any time for a line stop—and it can also be interrupted for correcting defectives. While the rate is not important, the daily schedule is, and if there are numerous line stops and reworks to perform, the workers may need to stay late to meet the daily schedule.

Any backtrack handling that is necessary is thought to be well worth it to be assured that the workers have a full measure of responsibility for quality. Actually the volume of rework is very small in Japanese plants these days, since many processes have defects rates as low as parts per million. Furthermore, Japanese just-in-time production keeps lots small, so that when defectives are detected there may be only one.

100 Percent Check

The sixth principle, 100 percent check, means inspection of every item, not just a random sample. The principle is intended to apply rigidly to finished goods, and where feasible to component parts.

If it is not feasible to check every component part—e.g., too expensive to do so manually, and technologically forbidding to perform automatically—then it is possible to rely on $N = 2$, which is discussed later in the "Techniques and Aids" section of this chapter. The long-range goal is to make changes that *will* make it feasible to do a 100 percent check of component parts.

Finished-goods inspection is where the Japanese approach most significantly departs from Western practices. Drawing a statistical sample and judging the whole lot according to the quality of the sample is standard procedure in the West. It is known as lot-acceptance sampling. Statistical sampling from a lot became widespread during World War II, when the U.S. armed services required suppliers to sample using government-furnished sampling tables. Today, virtually all quality control textbooks include MIL–STD–105D, which is the most popular of the World War II–vintage statistical sampling tables, and there are international equivalents of the tables.

Japanese industry learned about MIL–STD–105D and other U.S. Department of Defense tables in the postwar occupation by Allied troops. The U.S. military was the teacher. Some say that these events triggered the QC movement in Japan and the invitations to Deming and Juran to come to Japan and "tell us more."[4]

Sampling tables and lot-acceptance-sampling inspections are no longer viewed favorably in Japan. In the Japanese view lot-acceptance inspection has three strikes against it:

1. The very notion of a lot is in opposition to the low-inventory, just-in-time approach. It is preferable to inspect right away, piece by piece, so that defects are caught in time to correct the problem and avoid production of a whole lot of defectives.

2. The sampling tables require, as an input, the acceptable quality level (AQL) expressed in a percentage of defectives, i.e., defectives per 100 units. The Japanese now talk of defects in parts per million (PPM) and reject the notion of any *level* of defects being acceptable, which translates into rejection of the sampling tables.

3. To those who are really serious about quality, sampling itself is considered inadequate. An effort should be made to inspect every piece.

Project-by-Project Improvement

The final basic principle, project-by-project improvement, was alluded to earlier. The discussion of easy-to-see quality referred to display boards, found all over Japanese plants, which often mention the current quality improvement projects going on in the work area associated with the display. The displays also may list quality improvement projects that have been completed in the work area—a type of quality improvement scoreboard.

A particularly impressive example of such displays of QC project activities is in a Nihon Radiator Co. plant that I visited. The plant is a major supplier of radiators, mufflers, tail pipes, and automobile air-conditioners, particularly for Nissan. The QC project activities are a special source of pride for Mr. S. Kawanabe, who arranged to have the projects documented in the form of a 122-page booklet replete with diagrams, tables, and photos of project participants.

The Western visitor's reaction to QC project displays and booklets might be a mixture of admiration and skepticism—skepticism because keeping score on *number* of projects completed really cannot be considered as a valid measure of *degree* of quality improvement. While this is true, it is beside the point. The point is having a continual succession of quality improvement projects in every work area, year after year. The habit of annual improvement is at stake, and that is more important in Japanese TQC than is precise scorekeeping on who has improved how much.

That is not to say that no one is concerned about the extent of quality improvement. Typically the Japanese company has some sort of committee to review proposed quality improvement projects. The best are selected and assigned to project teams to be worked on in the next year.

Facilitating Concepts

Once the responsibility for quality is properly placed and basic quality control principles are put into effect, management should enhance the quality improvement effect by means of the five facilitating concepts listed under category 4 in Figure 3–1. The five concepts are: quality control as facilitator, small lot sizes, housekeeping, less-than-full-capacity scheduling, and daily machine checking.

Quality Control as Facilitator

What does the QC department do when primary responsibility for quality is assigned to the production department? Japan's answer is to make QC a facilitator. The QC department, much reduced in size, promotes the removal of defect causes, keeps track of quality accomplishments, monitors operations to see that standard procedures are followed, joins with purchasing people to similarly monitor supplier plant procedures, and coordinates QC training. Selecting parts to be inspected is no longer a QC department role. However, QC may be asked—by production—to perform some of the more complex or technical inspections: chemical lab work, destructive "torture" testing, total performance checks, and so forth.

QC people may serve as teachers and disseminators of QC information, but this function should not be so extensive that QC people become the recognized quality experts. Production has the primary responsibility for quality, and production foremen should be the quality experts. As has been mentioned, a widely circulated quality control journal for foremen has been published since 1962. In some plants foremen take engineering degrees; in plants that don't encourage outside education for foremen there

64

often is extensive education and training provided by corporate headquarters. The giant Matsushita manufacturing conglomerate maintains that type of management development center (patterned, perhaps, after the General Motors Institute).

The role of the QC department varies a good deal from one Japanese company to another. Nearly all companies would agree that the role must be that of facilitator. Actual practices differ, especially in regard to how much inspecting the QC people do. It appears that QC inspectors, if any, are most likely to be found after final assembly. One reason is that a 100 percent check of overall product performance is required, and such overall measures of quality are not easily assignable to a single work group in the production department. Similarly, some characteristics of the end products may need to be chemically analyzed, and a portion of a product may be torture-tested in a destructive testing procedure—both of which require special testing labs, equipment, and skills that the production people may want QC to handle.

One type of inspection that Western QC departments do a lot of and Japanese try to do none of (except for new suppliers) is receiving inspection. Receiving inspection means inspecting quality of goods coming in from other plants. By taking care of quality at the source, Japanese industry has, over the years, been able to phase out the need for receiving inspections. Supplier certification of quality is often extensive enough that parts may go directly from receiving docks to production, without pause for inspection or storage—the just-in-time mode of handling incoming materials.

At Kawasaki's Nebraska plant, quality control inspectors do perform receiving inspections, but only for parts and material purchased from U.S. suppliers. Sixty-five percent of Kawasaki's street bike parts are shipped in from Kawasaki, Japan, mostly in lot multiples of 200, but these lots are *not* inspected. Since Kawasaki, Japan, employs rigid process controls, the parts it makes for export to Nebraska can be counted on to be of exceptional quality, so that they need not be inspected. As the saying goes,

"You can't inspect quality in," and if there is thorough process control at the source, you don't have to try.

Small Lot Sizes

Small lot sizes are the key to just-in-time production. But as the previous chapter emphasized, small lot sizes are equally vital for assuring that defectives are caught early—before whole bad lots can be produced.

In my visits to manufacturing companies in Japan, I heard quality control department people asserting that small lot sizes are a basic concept or rule of quality control. And, of course, I also heard production people referring to small lot sizes as a key to just-in-time production. Clearly, small lot sizes are a vital ingredient in both the quality and the productivity components of the Japanese success formula.

Housekeeping

The Japanese are a tidy people. The streets are mostly free of trash, subway station walls are not marred by graffiti, shoes are removed before entering homes and temples, and hot towels are served before meals so that diners may clean their hands and faces. It is no surprise to find that Japanese factories are similarly neat and clean.

Safety is one reason for keeping factories tidy. Safety departments in Western companies have preached tidiness for years. Pride is a second reason. Military commanders conduct meticulous barracks inspections and examinations of personal grooming—in the expectation that the troops will come to feel that theirs is a "sharp outfit."

Quality control is perhaps the chief reason for good housekeeping in Japanese plants, but safety and pride undoubtedly are important related factors (intervening variables). We may expect that sloppy housekeeping habits encourage sloppy work habits, which lead to personal injury and injury to products and equipment. Conversely, good housekeeping should provide an environment conducive to improved work habits, quality, and care of facilities.

Inasmuch as good housekeeping is considered a contributor to good quality, housekeeping responsiblity must reside with those who have quality responsibility, namely, the foremen and workers. Usually Japanese workers, not an outside janitorial staff, keep their own work spaces tidy. But, as is discussed in another chapter, the just-in-time system requires workers to be very flexible. It is quite common for production workers who are temporarily not needed in their primary jobs to be assigned janitorial and other duties anywhere in the plant.

One example of the Japanese attention to neatness involves the Sanyo TV manufacturing plant in Arkansas. According to Harvard casewriters, when Sanyo took over the plant, which had faltered to the point of failure under U.S. ownership (and the Warwick name):

> One of the new management's first actions [to attack the quality problem] was to clear out the plant over a weekend, clean it and polyurethane the floors. Not only did this make the whole plant look cleaner and brighter, but it also reduced the dust in the air which sometimes caused equipment to gum up or interfered with the connections of electronic parts. "Also, when a floor is clean like that, anything that falls on it is more visible, so you automatically pick it up. It seems like a silly little thing, but it made a noticeable improvement in morale," remembered one man.[5]

A severe quality problem in the Warwick TV plant was corrected in a brief time by Sanyo management. Sanyo believes, and I see no reason to doubt it, that cleaning up the plant was an important contributing factor.

I have been in plenty of spic-and-span plants run by Americans, and so I am certainly not implying that the Japanese have a

67

monopoly on the plant-cleanliness idea. However, I have been in a number of dreadfully messy U.S. plants, too. If U.S. industry and Western industry generally are to match the Japanese in quality control, the housekeeping concept should be taken as a prerequisite.

Less-Than-Full-Capacity Scheduling

Less-than-full-capacity scheduling helps assure that the daily schedule will be met. It is also a quality control concept. For one thing, the concept makes it feasible to stop the line for quality or other problems (the line-stop principle). Furthermore, less-than-full-capacity scheduling avoids pressuring workers—and overtaxing equipment, tools, and support people—and thereby avoids errors in quality that could arise from haste. Preventing errors serves to decrease the need for line stops. Equally important, error prevention smooths the output rate, which makes it more feasible to operate without large inventory buffers between successive processes: the just-in-time ideal.

Daily Machine Checking

The last of the facilitating concepts, daily machine checking, is discussed in more detail in a later chapter dealing with production-line management. Suffice it to say here that while Western manufacturers tend to give their equipment hard use and overrely on the maintenance department, Japanese production workers pamper their machines. For example, first thing each morning the machine operator may go through a checklist, assuring that a number of machine functions are OK. Oiling, adjusting, tightening, sharpening, and so on would precede the start of work.

Daily machine checking seems natural to workers whose first priority is quality, because faulty machines are often the cause of defectives. While some Western workers follow a similar regimen, the tendency is toward laxity.

Techniques and Aids

Western quality control practices are based on few principles and facilitating concepts, relying instead mostly on specialists employing various techniques and aids. In Japanese TQC, techniques and aids have a lesser but still valuable role. The TQC techniques and aids are mostly different from those used in Western industry. As shown in category 5 of Figure 3–1, they include: exposure of problems, foolproof devices, $N = 2$, analysis tools, and quality control circles.

Exposure of Problems

A defective, in the TQC system, engenders mixed emotions: remorse over the error, but some cheer over the exposure of one more problem to solve. The defective part triggers a thorough investigation to root out the cause forever.

In the Japanese system, rooting out causes is valued to the point where management may deliberately remove workers or buffer inventories so that problems in maintaining quality and meeting the schedule are exposed. This was explained in the Chapter 2 discussion of the JIT/TQC cause-effect model (Figure 2–4). Exposing problems and correcting causes may also be accomplished simply by looking for them—*before* there is evidence of trouble. This is a suitable endeavor for workers to pursue during slack time and in small group improvement activities or quality control circles. Other staff, especially engineers, may search for hidden problems as part of their normal daily activities, e.g., while working on product or process designs.

69

Foolproof Devices

Human beings will always make mistakes, but the work process can be designed to eliminate many of them. Thus, the idea of making the process somewhat foolproof has become basic in Japanese TQC. Devices called *bakayoke* may be attached to machines to automatically check for abnormals in a process. At Toyota these are called autonomous machines. According to Monden, "In Toyota factories, almost all machines are autonomous, so that mass production of defects can be prevented and machine breakdowns autonomously checked."[6] The monitoring mechanisms thus may check for causal factors like malfunction and tool wear, as well as measuring dimensions of produced parts and warning when tolerances are coming close to being exceeded. Such QC devices are virtually essential in companies that are to achieve quality levels measured in defective parts per million. (Some *bakayoke* automatically shut off a machine when the required number of parts have been made, an inventory control element of just-in-time production.)

Foolproof devices to check every piece are especially suitable for production of component parts. *Bakayoke* are sometimes used in final assembly, especially in the more automated assembly tasks. For manual assembly—the dominant mode—workers may stop the line or turn on a yellow warning light when they see something wrong. The buttons that activate the lights may be considered surrogates for foolproof devices.

$N = 2$

Foolproof devices are most feasible for high-volume operations. In lower-volume production, where such devices are not presently affordable, human inspection is required. A high percentage, perhaps even 100 percent, are inspected if the process is considered unstable, i.e., the part hasn't been made often enough to work the bugs out of the process. Relating the quantity to be inspected to the level of instability is a Western QC practice that the Japanese accept. For more stable processes it may be safe to inspect by sampling, and to Western QC people the *random* sample is basic.

Actually, Western quality control books and manuals—those that are carefully worded, at least—advocate *representative* sampling. And "representative," in Japanese TQC, now means the first piece and the last piece, *not* a random selection. The first and last pieces constitute a sample size of two, hence the name "$N = 2$." In a stable process, the Japanese reason, the first and last pieces encompass the entire production run, but a random sample in a typical Western sample size of $N = 5$ does not. In the $N = 2$ approach, if the first and last pieces are good it is assumed that the process has remained stable (e.g., no tool wear or out-of-adjustment conditions have arisen) and therefore all parts are good.

Tools of Analysis

Problems exposed are candidates for investigation and analysis. Problem analysis tools include quality dispersion charts (frequency distributions of measured quality variables), defect frequency rates and trends, and process control charts (with upper and lower control limits to show statistical severity of quality deviations). These statistical tools are well known to journeyman QC people in Western industry. In Japan, many supervisors and workers have even been trained in their use.

A tool of analysis that was largely unknown in Western industry until recently is the Ishikawa diagram, a cause-and-effect display tool more popularly known as the "fishbone" chart because of its shape. Figure 3–2 is an example. Fishbone-chart analysis begins with selection of a quality problem to work on. In

Figure 3–2, "fracture surface of cast metal" is the quality problem, and it is listed to the right of the main arrow. Workers, supervisors, engineers, and others then determine the chief factors that affect the quality characteristics being investigated. In Japan, the factors may be determined in informal sessions late in the workday if the day's schedule has been met early; sometimes the determination takes place in formally constituted quality control circles or small group improvement activities.

The factors that are thought to be most critical are written on the main lines of the fishbone. In Figure 3–2 these include mold temperature, mold coating, casting temperature, and composition of molten metal. Subfactors are listed on the secondary lines; for example, for mold temperature, casting interval and casting volume are subfactors written on secondary lines.

The completed fishbone chart may be enlarged and hung out in the plant to keep people at the work site aware of causes and effects. An effect, i.e., a quality characteristic or problem—fracture surface of cast metal in this case—is carefully evaluated during production; efforts to improve that characteristic or to

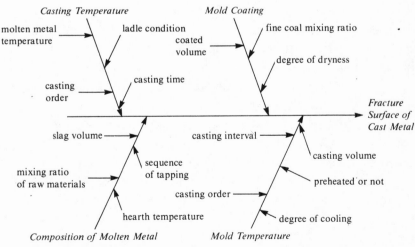

Figure 3–2. Fishbone Diagram (Japan Industrial Standard Z–8101)

72

cope with a quality decrease may be focused on the factors and subfactors displayed on the fishbone chart.

QC Circles

Quality control circles are listed last among the 20 TQC concepts from Figure 3–1. That does not mean least important, but rather it emphasizes my belief that QC circles should be considered as a good way of wringing some of the last defects out of the production system. If QC circles are established early with the expectation of being the company's quality control salvation, disappointment will surely result. (Some Western companies have instituted quality circle programs that aim at morale-improving suggestions, which is probably a reasonable expectation with which I would have no quarrel.) In view of the great Western interest in circles, a full chapter is devoted to the subject later in the book.

Getting TQC Started in the United States

Our discussion of 20 quality control concepts in 5 categories may have succeeded in conveying the idea of *total* quality control. Yet there is another sense to the word "total" in the Japanese system: *total involvement,* meaning a sharing in the quality control responsibility by all plant employees. Production has primary responsiblity, but the solution of quality problems requires close interaction between production people and others, especially manufacturing engineers, QC department staff, purchasing people, maintenance people, production control people, and design engineers. All should be involved in quality improvement projects at all times, and they should be ready to respond quickly to breakdowns, deliberate line stops, and other irregular problem events. (The idea of total involvement is nicely conveyed by the term "company-wide quality control," CWQC. Some Japanese prefer CWQC over the term "total quality control," because they want to avoid any confusion with TQC in the limited U.S. sense of the term. I prefer TQC, because I want to encompass not just the involvement but also the concepts, techniques, and so forth.)

Also, all levels of management should be closely involved. At the Gunma plant of Nihon Radiator Co. in Japan, the plant manager, who led me on a tour, pointed out that he was particularly interested in all of the QC projects on plant display boards that were designated with red adhesive dots. The dots told the project participants to give those projects high priority.

It is easy enough for Western managers to reassign primary QC responsibility to production, but the idea that a key responsibility is to be assigned and also shared is quite another matter. Akio Morita, the chief executive officer in Sony Corp., stated:

> When we opened our San Diego plant, we really had some difficulty persuading our American engineers and managers to go onto the production floor and mingle with the foremen and workers to learn how things were really being made. Without knowing how things were made, how can you design quality into new products and design out product defects?[7]

TQC in Japanese-owned U.S. Electronics Plants

Stories like Sony's have also emerged from the other two Japanese TV/electronics plants in the United States: Quasar (owned by Matsushita) and Sanyo. According to Juran, prior to Japanese ownership and the Quasar name, the Motorola plant had 150 to 180 defects per 100 TV sets. Three years later, under Japanese ownership, the defect rate was only 3 or 4 per 100 TVs, about a fortyfold improvement.[8] Similar reports have been published regarding Sanyo's takeover of the Warwick TV plant in Arkansas.

We may examine these reports to see how far Sanyo was able to go toward implementing total quality control with a U.S. work force.

The floundering Warwick TV-manufacturing plant in Forrest City, Arkansas, was bought by Sanyo in 1977. Sales of Warwick's color television sets had declined so steeply that 80 percent of plant capacity was shut down. Sears, Roebuck and Co. had been buying most of Warwick's TVs under the Sears label, and Sears owned 25 percent of Warwick's stock. But the quality had declined to the point where Sears was buying mostly from Japanese manufacturers.

Within about two months of taking over the plant, according to one report, Sanyo had cut the "product defect rate from about 30 percent to less than 5 percent . . . without making any substantial changes in the factory's manufacturing equipment."[9] Nor were employees fired. Mostly the same employees and managers who had been there under Warwick were achieving the improvements in quality.

One important exception: The former chief of quality control was made plant manager, a move that clearly announced Sanyo's commitment to quality—as a line function, not a staff function.[10] With QC responsibility reassigned to production, the new Japanese managers did not approve of most of the old QC department inspection practices. Mr. Takemoto, Sanyo's vice chairman, recalls:

> The American managers were proudly pointing out to me the spacious, well-equipped and well-staffed quality inspection section at the end of the assembly line. I wondered why they needed such an elaborate quality inspection station if they made their products properly in the first place. I told our workers to properly and carefully complete the assigned job, and not to send any slipshod work down the assembly line. In this way we cut the defect rate drastically.[11]

The talk about quality was accompanied by actions to achieve it. Higher standards for quality were established, and

75

new equipment and new procedures were provided to help meet the standards. According to one employee:

> In the Warwick days, volume and cost were all-important. If we had a quality problem and I wanted to put some additional people on the line, the line managers would fight me. They were under orders to keep their costs down. If a snag develops on the line today, we put more people on it right away and don't worry about the cost. I don't think [one of the Japanese managers] even knows what a labor utilization sheet is.[12]

That does not mean that productivity and cost were neglected. New assembly procedures cut the assembly cycle time per worker substantially. Producing goods faster does not clash with the goal of quality but contributes to it, because feedback and response to defects is that much faster—a just-in-time effect.

TQC in Japanese-owned U.S. Automotive Plants

While the electronics industry competes mostly on the basis of quality, the automotive industry competes on the basis of price and quality, perhaps in that order. Perhaps that helps explain why we are mostly hearing about quality improvement in Japanese-owned U.S. television plants, whereas the just-in-time-production stories come from Japanese-owned plants in the U.S. automotive industry.

So far, such automotive plants are limited to the Kawasaki and Honda motorcycle plants and a few small Japanese plants supplying auto components and accessories, e.g., the TRI-CON subsidiary of Tokyo Seating Co. and the Calsonic subsidiary of Nihon Radiator Co. Honda and Nissan are starting up automobile assembly plants in the United States, and a host of other Japanese supplier plants are planning their own American subsidiary plants; the pace of implementing TQC and JIT in this country should pick up accordingly, especially since Nissan and Honda are among Japan's innovators in the TQC and JIT areas.

76

At the Kawasaki motorcycle plant in Nebraska the early emphasis has been on developing the just-in-time system, but a few TQC features are in evidence. For one thing, each time I visit the plant I notice more "easy-to-see quality," mainly blackboards and other displays in the work areas. So far, the display boards do not tell of current or completed quality improvement projects, nor do they single out people or work groups for special recognition. Instead the displays are used by workers and supervisors to enter hourly production statistics and also to tally types of problems. There is no particular distinction between delays and quality problems. Both are recorded, and the frequency of occurrences of a given problem may suggest corrective action: training, redesign, better tool maintenance, suggestions to a supplier of material, and so forth.

The Kawasaki plant also follows the Japanese TQC pattern of not scheduling at full capacity. A good share of the time, the production lines will have a good day and reach the day's scheduled output with work time to spare. When that happens, workers and supervisors can use the time to discuss what things have gone wrong recently, as recorded on blackboards. Ideas for corrective action may be generated, and various tools for analyzing quality problems may be used.

The other notable TQC measures in use are minimum lot sizes, line stop, foolproof devices, exposure of problems, and process control. Lot sizes are under steady attack in all processes, from purchased parts to made parts to subassemblies and final assemblies. Specifics are included in the next chapter.

Line stop, by means of switches within reach of final-assembly workers, has been mentioned. The switches (surrogate foolproof devices) turn on yellow or red lights, which signal a warning or stop the line, respectively.

At a sister motorcycle plant run by Kawasaki in Japan, I saw a more sophisticated line apparatus. Instead of yellow and red light bulbs, there are lighted displays about the size of some basketball scoreboards. This is a Toyota type of display (called an *andon*), and it includes a row of numbers that light up to signal which work area is having the trouble. Furthermore, a special clock at the end of the line records the cumulative number of minutes that the line has been stopped during the day. Photos of the *andon* and the clock are shown in Figures 3–3 and 3–4.

The Kawasaki, Nebraska, plant exposes problems by removing workers from the line until the yellow warning lights come on, which is the sign that workers cannot keep up without making mistakes. The sources of the likely mistakes are unearthed for intensive study and improvement. The lights and problem exposure policy are more fully described in the next chapter.

Process control at Kawasaki, Nebraska, has been only partially implemented. Production supervisors understand that quality is to be mostly their responsibility, but the quality control department still has several inspectors and has a good deal of

Figure 3–3. Andon at Kawasaki Motors, Akashi, Japan

Figure 3–4. Line-Stop Clock at Kawasaki Motors, Akashi, Japan

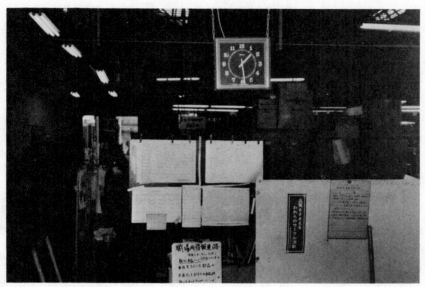

influence. Also, foremen and workers lack training in QC and in process control.

It is probably in the purchasing area where process control of quality is most pronounced. Kawasaki buyers, design engineers, and QC people spend a good deal of time in suppliers' plants and on the phone helping the suppliers to improve their own process controls. The hope is that the suppliers' quality will improve enough so that Kawasaki QC people will no longer need to conduct receiving inspections of incoming lots. That would get Kawasaki out of the lot-inspection mode entirely, so that all efforts could be concentrated on process controls. Furthermore, the size—and influence—of the QC department could decrease appreciably, since about two-thirds of the QC inspectors are presently assigned to receiving inspections, which would no longer be needed. Probably most of Kawasaki's U.S. suppliers follow the American practice of not welcoming advice from customer plants. But Kawasaki buyers are hard at work trying to

79

convince the suppliers of the logic of Japanese-style close cooperation between suppliers and customers. These and other points are examined in detail in a later chapter devoted to just-in-time purchasing.

Employee Involvement and Training

Training may be the biggest hurdle in the way of significant changes with respect to quality in Western industry. It is a problem for the Japanese subsidiaries like Kawasaki, but a greater one for Western-owned companies. Juran feels that it will not be possible for the West to catch up with Japanese quality before the end of the decade because of the time it takes to train everybody. He notes that Japanese industry's massive quality-training program included "hundreds of thousands of managers and supervisors at all organization levels and in all company departments, plus millions of nonsupervisors." But it took an entire decade—until the 1960s—to train the upper and middle managers. Only then did the training of foremen and workers begin.[13]

Plantwide training in quality control was virtually unheard of in Western industry—until recently. Nashua Corp. may be the first exception. A few years ago William Conway, Nashua's chief executive officer, hired W. Edwards Deming as a quality control consultant. As a result Nashua instituted a program of top-to-bottom training in quality control, with a strong emphasis on problem detection through use of statistical techniques.

The Nashua approach to quality control is explained by Conway in two 30-minute videotapes that have been widely played in some large U.S. corporations. For example, the videotape has been viewed in many plants of Control Data Corp. And some Control Data plants have already implemented extensive changes to upgrade this approach to quality. The key change that has been made is assignment of responsibility for quality to production, so that actual inspections are generally not performed any longer by the QC department. QC's new, more limited role is to conduct quality audits for production.

Most other Western companies have not yet taken meaningful steps to improve quality—though awareness of the need to do so is widespread. There simply has been too little convincing information about what to do, and all too many Western companies have been sidetracked into thinking—or hoping—that quality circles would do the trick. For the most part, getting out the product and cutting costs are still ahead of improving quality in the list of priorities of most of our industrial firms.

The Time Is Ripe

I am less pessimistic than Juran. Yes, top-to-bottom quality consciousness took two decades to achieve in Japan. But Japan began with perhaps the world's worst quality. Furthermore, the Japanese have *learned how* to effectively turn bad quality into good quality, and they have performed the miracle in U.S. electronics plants with U.S. workers in short order. In addition, good quality is not expensive—as Philip Crosby maintains in the title of his fine little book *Quality is Free*.[14] (While TQC involves little startup cost, JIT may require an initial outlay for engineering and toolmaking to cut setup times.)

Actually quality is better than free; *quality is productivity,* because so many costs—rework, scrap, inspection, customer returns, and so forth—are avoided each time a quality improvement is effected. As William Conway, chief executive officer at Nashua Corp., puts it:

> As quality goes up, so does productivity. Consider the impact on overall levels of productivity if everyone and every machine in your company performed properly the first time, every time. The same number of employees would be handling much larger volumes of work. The high cost of inspec-

tion would be directed into productive activities. Rework, downgrading, scrapping would be eliminated. Administrative efficiency would be much higher.[15]

Western consumers have become quality-conscious, manufacturing managers are eager to respond to the Japanese quality challenge, and we know how to proceed. Dramatic results are possible in *this* decade.

So the time is ripe for a quality revolution in Western industry. The recommended course of action, based on the points of this chapter, may be expressed in this restatement of lesson 3:

Production, not quality control, must have primary responsibility for quality; and everybody, including top management, must participate in project-by-project quality improvement.

CHAPTER 4

The Debut of Just-in-Time Production in the United States

LESSON 4: Culture is no obstacle; techniques can change behavior.

In one sense it is a bit early to write about just-in-time manufacturing management in the United States. JIT has scarcely been tested here, and what few examples there are have too brief a history to offer conclusive guidance on how to adapt Japanese JIT to the American environment.

On the other hand, the Japanese already have at least ten years' head start—and much more if one considers Japan's long history of adaptation to its environment of resource scarcities. It is time for Western manufacturers to take the JIT plunge. While there are not many JIT companies outside of Japan, one plant, Kawasaki's Lincoln, Nebraska, subsidiary, has had a full-fledged JIT program since 1980; and while Kawasaki (like most private corporations) does not welcome close public scrutiny, enough is known about its JIT history for the Kawasaki case to be considered as a fairly rich source of information. The just-in-time discussion in this chapter consists of JIT applications *within* the factory. The external element of the JIT system, just-in-time purchasing, is treated in a full chapter later in the book. The JIT purchasing chapter examines applications in Kawasaki and a few other Japanese subsidiaries in the United States, plus the beginnings of a JIT purchasing movement among American-owned companies.

Kawasaki, U.S.A., Under American Management

In 1975 Kawasaki Heavy Industries (KHI) opened a plant in Lincoln, Nebraska, to manufacture motorcycles, and later snowmobiles, jet skis, and a special balloon-tired three-wheel motorcycle for the U.S. recreational market. American managers and American workers were hired to operate the plant. A few experienced Japanese from KHI in Japan were assigned to the Lincoln plant in advisory roles. In hiring American managers, KHI got American management techniques and customs—warts and all.

The Lincoln plant had three different plant managers in less than four years, but the birth pangs may have been more or less normal and not particularly worthy of our attention. It was the third plant manager, Dennis Butt, who, with the support and urging of the Japanese advisers and KHI headquarters, launched the just-in-time production management program. Butt is no longer plant manager. In September 1981 he was replaced by a Japanese plant manager in a reorganization that included adding two more Japanese managers and eliminating several managerial positions. The reasons for the reorganization have not been made public and perhaps are not of special concern to us anyway. The JIT program *was* begun under Butt, a non-Japanese manager, and it is instructive to examine how.

Rejecting MRP

Before becoming plant manager at Kawasaki, Butt was a materials manager at Eagle Signal, an electric products manufacturer owned by Gulf and Western. In that position, he was instrumental in implementing material requirements planning (MRP) systems in the industrial division of Gulf and Western plants. MRP harnesses computer power to plan for the right parts to be available at the right time. Inasmuch as the Kawasaki operation at that time was plagued with problems of having too much inventory overall but running out of the parts that were needed, MRP seemed to be the answer. By late 1979, a reported $300,000 had been spent on MRP preparation, including training.[1]

In the meantime, Butt had been learning about a Japanese alternative to MRP: a kanban-based JIT system, which KHI had been perfecting in its Japanese plants. A team of experts from Japan visited Kawasaki's Lincoln plant in early 1980 and succeeded in persuading Butt to abandon the MRP project. One reason was that the Lincoln plant needed a quick fix, and the simplicity of kanban was attractive as compared with the years and cost (an estimated $1 million overall) it would take to fully implement MRP.

Butt became a strong kanban advocate, partly because he was able to prove to himself that the kanban system has sound theoretical roots, based on cutting setup times and lot sizes. Butt had studied operations research (mathematical modeling for managerial decision making) in college, and he developed graphic explanations of the effects of cutting setup times (EOQ graphs as in Figure 2–2). Kawasaki's management team learned about kanban with reference to Butt's graphs. Today if you were to interview one of the young American managers at the Kawasaki plant about the way its system works, chances are that your interviewee would drag out pencil and paper and begin drawing those before-and-after EOQ graphs.

85

It is worth mentioning that Butt started out believing that he should have "old war-horses" in key production positions. He changed his mind. Several old-timers were replaced with young, pliable people, who did not find it so hard to accept new ideas. They came to accept the Japanese approach, at least to the degree necessary to make some progress. Old war-horses often find it tough to accept MRP, much less so radically different an approach as JIT.

Trying to Use Kanban

Initially, Butt and his staff thought they were trying to implement kanban, which was the term being used by the KHI people. *Kanban* is a Japanese word meaning "visible record," and in the kanban system a manually prepared card, or kanban, is the visible record that triggers an order for more parts. The tie-in with setup time and lot size is this: If a kanban arrives at a work center signaling the need for more of a given part, that part is needed right away. It must be possible to set up for the part fast enough to economically make the very small quantity required; other work centers will send more kanban to signal the need for other parts, and numerous new setups will be required each day as the kanban arrive. (Kanban is more fully explained in the appendix.)

Kawasaki's first kanban attempt linked the motorcycle final assembly line with a supply point providing some 400 kinds of "hardware": washers, grommets, nuts, screws, and so forth. This attempt at kanban did not seem to solve problems, seemed to lack purpose, and was run without proper discipline. It was abandoned within a few weeks.

Early Successes

Actually, the abortive kanban experiment was just one of several measures undertaken at the plant in the spring of 1981. The other

86

measures, which were generally successful, had about the same objective as the use of kanban: to improve productivity by tighter controls on inventories. By that time, the term "just-in-time" was coming into use in the United States among those studying the trickle of information available on Japanese manufacturing.[2] Butt and his managers came to understand that the overall goal of productivity improvement translated into a just-in-time operating objective; kanban was just one of several tools for moving toward the JIT operating objective.

All of the Kawasaki managers were challenged to develop ways to cut inventories and move toward just-in-time operations. The purchasing manager trained all of his buyers in JIT purchasing, and the buyers in turn worked on ways to effect small, more frequent deliveries of bought materials. Within the plant, punch presses were outfitted with platforms made of roller conveyors so that heavy dies could be changed in minutes rather than hours. A welding shop was converted from a general-purpose welding booth configuration to several welding production lines, each dedicated to welding frames for a certain size of motorcycle, with frames moving piece by piece down the welding lines. A differential subassembly shop was physically moved to a position where it could feed differentials "just-in-time" to the using station on the assembly line for three-wheel motorcycles. The receiving procedure for parts coming from Japan was changed to a dock-to-line flow pattern, which eliminated 60 percent of the storage racks, and the space was turned over to manufacturing.

Plant Vision

These improvements all occurred in the space of a few months in spring 1981, which was about a year after Kawasaki's decision to abandon MRP in favor of kanban and related Japanese approaches. While these improvements were taking shape, Dennis Butt was trying to rationalize and articulate the overall JIT effort.

87

Butt came up with the following statement. *"I envision the entire plant as a series of stations on the assembly line, whether physically there or not."*

This "plant vision," as we might call it, became about as familiar to line managers and professional staff as Butt's EOQ charts.[3] The Kawasaki "dog-and-pony show" for visiting delegations from other U.S. companies invariably included both the charts and the plant-vision statement.

There may be something unique about Butt's plant vision. The simplicity and clarity of the statement may have helped achieve unified purpose, which is a rare phenomenon in American organizations. We tend to organize our analysts and decision makers by function or specialty, with the result that functional goals and personal career paths often conflict with the good of the whole organization.[4] Kawasaki, Lincoln, is organized like that: industrial engineers in an IE department, inspectors in a quality control department, maintenance people in a maintenance department, and so forth. But the plant-vision concept exhorts all managers, whether staff or line, to work toward integrating the entire plant into a vast production line, which, as we shall see in a later chapter, is the type of plant configuration needed to support just-in-time production.

Achieving Consensus

Most reports on Japanese industry in the popular and the business press give special emphasis to Japanese cultural attributes favoring consensus-based decision making. The Japanese tendency is to allow plenty of time for all affected parties to have meaningful inputs when alternatives are being evaluated. The process of reaching consensus tends to be agonizingly slow—by Western standards. But the happy end result is a decision that is quickly and smoothly implemented.

Does Kawasaki, Lincoln, employ Japanese-style consensus

processes? Naturally, no. How could it? The people involved are Americans brought up in the individualistic American environment. Kawasaki's decision processes are typically American. An individual who comes up with a promising idea tries to steamroll the idea as far as it will go and as fast as possible.

In most U.S. organizations the casualty rate of abandoned ideas is high. Time is not taken to gain consensus. Therefore:

1. Many doubters remain, and they passively or actively resist.

2. Issues outside the area of expertise of the innovator are not properly considered, which makes the decision somewhat prone to failure, whether there is resistance or not.

Individualistic decision processes are not all bad, and consensus processes are not all good. Folklore tells us that groups stifle creativity.[5] The Japanese have been accused of being poor innovators, which our folkloric perceptions about groups would predict. But sheer engineering power and very high literacy may make Japan an innovative leader, as well as the world's preeminent copier, in spite of group-think.

In the case of Kawasaki, the outside observer gets the impression of a higher than average success rate for the innovations that make it to the implementation stage. Of the JIT program projects that have been mentioned, there was the kanban failure but several notable successes.

There are a few reasons why we might expect Kawasaki's JIT project success rate to be good:

1. With such a clear, unifying overall plant objective—the plant vision—there is not a great deal of room for an individual or a department to pursue an objective that is out of phase with the JIT wishes of the plant manager. Perhaps there is a management principle here that Chester I. Barnard[6] might have agreed with: *If there is consensus with regard to objective, the process of reaching the objective is inconsequential.*

2. KHI has staffed its Lincoln plant on the lean side. That is, there are not a lot of white-collar staff specialists who might erect roadblocks. Or, putting it more positively, the foremen on the Kawasaki shop floor are vested with more responsibility than in the typical U.S. plant, where shop-related responsibilities are shared by a broad variety of line and staff parties. (But compared with Japanese plants, Kawasaki, Lincoln, still is staff-heavy.)

Other Plant Visions

Kawasaki seems to get unified action by emphasizing an ideal plant configuration. In the previous chapter we examined the case of Sanyo's TV plant in Arkansas, and we might infer that there a plant vision emphasizing high quality was a unifying force. In still other plants, management might get results—i.e., levels of performance that are competitive with those of similar plants in Japan—by emphasizing a particular inventory approach, or training, or equipment design. There are not many of these approaches that will be broad-based enough to effect plant-wide improvements. I am only saying that Kawasaki's approach is not the only one that will work well.

Kawasaki, U.S.A., Under Japanese Management

As has been mentioned, Dennis Butt is no longer the Kawasaki plant manager, as of September 1981. Also, a few other white-collar staff positions were eliminated when Japanese managers took over. But the JIT program continues, perhaps more vigorously than before. Three immediate JIT steps taken by Butt's Japanese replacements are:

1. Installation of trouble lights above the main motorcycle lines.

2. Preparation to run mixed models in final assembly.

3. Tearing down some of the parts-feeder conveyors.

Each of these steps is significant and far-reaching, as is explained below.

Trouble Lights

On the main motorcycle assembly line a yellow light has been installed above every work station (manned by one or more assemblers), and a red light has been mounted above every natural grouping of work stations. Switches hang down from cords at worker height. An assembler whose production has been slowed by some problem or who is not able to keep up with the speed of the line turns on the yellow light, which is the signal for a roving master assembler to come and help. Also the light alerts the supervisor to the problem. The red light is turned on only when a problem is severe enough to bring the line to a halt. Then master assemblers, supervisors, foremen, and all idled line workers help get the line going again.

The red light brings frowns, but plant management is pleased when many of the yellow lights are on. Yes, *on*. As one Kawasaki manager put it, ''When the yellow lights are on, that means we are really busting ass.'' To follow this reasoning, we must understand that the main reason for the yellow is too few workers on the line to handle the rate of output. If no yellow lights are on, management knows that the line is moving too slowly or there are too many workers. Usually, the response is to pull workers off the line and assign them elsewhere so that it becomes hard for the remaining workers to keep up; so yellow lights begin to come on. (If all are on, it is time for management to back off: Add back a few workers—or slow the speed of the line.) Pulling assemblers off the line exposes remaining assemblers and their supervisors to trouble, e.g., inability to keep up without sacrificing quality, which leads to an attack on the cause of the trouble—whether human or mechanical—so that it won't happen again. This idea, exposure of problems, was discussed in the previous chapter as a technique of Japanese total quality control.

Pulling assemblers off the assembly line is quite like removing buffer inventories between fabrication work stations, which was described in Chapter 2. The effect is constant improvement of productivity: the same or higher output with less and less material and labor input.

Speedup and the Labor Union

Removing workers from a production line is not a common management tactic in Western industry, but speeding up the line, which has similar results, is common enough. Workers call it "speedup," a word having strong negative connotations among Western labor unions. One might wonder about worker reactions to speedup induced by removal of assemblers at Kawasaki, Lincoln. The United Auto Workers have tried to organize the plant and so far have lost at the ballot box. But isn't the speedup tactic playing into the hands of the labor organizers? Time will tell. If Kawasaki's American workers do not object it will be because:

1. They know that such measures are necessary if the plant is to compete and survive.

2. It is apparent to those involved that the tactic is not so much a means of motivating labor as it is a way of exposing and solving the methods and facilities problems that would keep the work force from continually improving performance. By contrast, typical American uses of speedup tactics seem to have no purpose other than to drive the work force.

3. There surely is a considerable sense of pride and esprit de corps among a group of assembly-line workers who see their productivity go up, up, up as they pitch in to solve

92

the cause of yellow lights. Sustaining the habit of improvement, referred to in the last chapter, is its own reward. Inasmuch as assembly work is inherently boring, psychic rewards can make the difference.

Preparation for Mixed Models

The Kawasaki plant improvement timetable called for running "5–5" by early 1982—the same as in the mother plant at Akashi, Japan. What that means is assembling five units of one motorcycle model followed by five of the next model and so forth. This is not quite full mixed-model sequencing, but is close to it. In January 1982 the Lincoln plant converted, not to 5–5 but to 1–1, which is full mixed-model sequencing. (The plant in Akashi is now running 1–1 some of the time as well—perhaps in order not to be outdone by the Lincoln plant!)

An advantage of mixed-model sequencing is that each day you make close to the same mix of products that you sell that day. This avoids the usual cycle of a large buildup of inventory of a given model, followed by depletion to the point of potential lost sales as the next model builds up. Furthermore, when mixed models are run in final assembly, the same mixed-model schedule may (in a mature system) govern the making and delivering of component parts, ideally even from outside suppliers. Planning and control are simplified, capacity requirements are reduced, and buffer inventories are slashed—with all of the attendant quality and other just-in-time benefits.

The new Japanese management team began preparing for mixed models almost immediately after their arrival in Lincoln. The key preparatory steps involved redesigning parts locations and handling aids along the assembly line. Foremen, assemblers, materials control people, and industrial engineers aggressively attacked the problem of imprecise and inconvenient parts locations, which can slow down the assemblers, especially when changing from one model to another.

An important aid is color coding, which is widely used in Japan. Each model of motorcycle has an identifying color, and that color may be found on all cartons for parts, handling trays, feeder storage racks, and so forth. The ideal is zero time for a worker to hunt for the part needed—and also for the materials control people to hunt for the right location when restocking. An old slogan, "A place for everything, and everything in its place," applies.

This insistence upon precise placement of production materials made a particular impression on me. I was reminded of when, as a teenager, I worked one summer as a hod carrier and "mud man." For a time that summer I was assigned to deliver bricks and mix mortar (mud) for a bricklayer, who, I was told, was the fastest bricklayer in the state. He was nonunion and contracted to be paid by the brick. My job was to place the bricks so precisely that he could reach to the designated place and grab a brick without looking. Also, I was to keep his mud at the precise consistency that he wanted—by adding water and mixing as the heat dried the mortar out on his mud board. It is no wonder that he was fast; other bricklayers that I worked for later were four or five times slower because they turned around and looked for the next brick and also added their own water to the mud on their mud boards.

I don't believe that the champion bricklayer was more tired out at day's end than the slow bricklayers. Because the champion's materials were precisely provided, he was the very picture of economy of motion, a cherished tenet of Frederick Taylor and the other pioneers of scientific management. The champion did less bending, stooping, turning, and reaching. Similarly, precise placement and identification of parts for assembly-line workers may save them some motions and make the work less tiring.

Conveyor Removal

"The Japanese don't believe in conveyors," according to Ed Hay, materials manager of Fram Corp.[7] Hay had spent three weeks touring Japanese plants in the Toyota family, and his comment is intended to apply to materials handling between *manned* work stations. (The Japanese certainly *are* in favor of conveyors —actually automatic transfer devices—on *automated* production lines.) He found that the Toyota people believe that the best way to move parts is for one worker to physically hand a part to the next worker, or if the next worker's hands are busy, place the part on his bench.

One of the Kawasaki, Lincoln, managers said about the same thing: "The Japanese were big on conveyors about ten years ago; now they try to avoid them." The Kawasaki manager was explaining why, in fall 1981, two conveyor systems were no longer in use and were scheduled for removal. One of the conveyors fed mounted tires from a tire-mounting subassembly area overhead across the plant to the station on the motorcycle assembly line where tires were installed. The other conveyor fed gas tanks from tank fabrication overhead to the tank-installation station on the motorcycle line.

In spring 1981 Kawasaki managers had enjoyed showing off those conveyor systems, and the many visitors from other U.S. plants who came to tour Kawasaki surely approved of the conveyors, because they fitted our American notions of automation and assembly-line efficiency. The Japanese managers who took over in September did not approve. There are perhaps five reasons why:

1. *Inventory*. Conveyors hold inventory. Inventory costs money; delays feedback on quality, which leads to more scrap and rework and less quality consciousness; and is an administrative burden. Now tires are mounted directly adjacent to the station, where they are installed so that inventory is only one or two mounted tires.

2. *Quantities*. Quantity control is not precise when inventories are on moving conveyors. At any given time one might guess that there are 80 tires plus or minus 5, or 250 gas tanks plus or minus 10. A tenet of modern Japanese manufacturing management is plus or minus *zero*. Now gas tanks are loaded into racks

95

that are specially designed with compartments for exactly 40 tanks, 20 on each side. The racks are on rubber wheels so that one worker can easily push a full rack to final assembly when needed. Figures 4-1 and 4-2 show the new racks and the old conveyor.

3. *Flexibility.* Conveyors *push* inventory forward, whether needed or not. An important feature of the Japanese kanban system is use of the work center to *pull* inventory from the supply points as needed. The Kawasaki plant needs to prepare for the introduction of kanban by evolving toward simple, flexible ways to move parts, in response to a "pull" from the using work area. (The notification that corresponds to the pull is a card in the formal kanban system, but the concept applies as well if some other way of notification is used: An intercom, a flag, a wave, or a shout for more parts will do. One amusing but effective notification method in use at the Kawasaki plant in Akashi is golf balls: Several different colors of golf balls are on hand at one work

Figure 4-1. Rack for 40 Gas Tanks

Figure 4–2. Gas Tank Conveyor

station making several models of a motorcycle subassembly. When parts for a given model are running low, the operator drops a golf ball into a pipe; the ball rolls down the pipe to the work station where the parts are made, and the color of the ball signifies *which* model the parts are needed for.)

4. *Breakdowns*. Conveyors are subject to breakdown, a se-

rious concern in a JIT factory, in which there is little or no buffer inventory.

5. *Cost.* Conveyors are expensive to buy, install, maintain, and relocate.

Future Projects

Kawasaki, Lincoln, has a number of new just-in-time projects in progress, but at this point most are confidential. In the next chapter I will discuss one project that I believe is or will be underway, a project to emulate a change that is already in effect at the sister plant in Akashi, Japan. The example is of great interest to Western industry, because it dramatically demonstrates the tendency for Japanese manufacturers to make many of their own small, simple, lightweight machine tools. Such "homemade" tooling generally performs one task very well—and at far less cost than Western companies usually must pay for the typical large multipurpose equipment bought from machine-tool manufacturers.

Performance in a Recession

The just-in-time system enables manufacturing to react quickly to changes in the mix of products and models sold in the marketplace—providing that the company has labor flexibility so that employees may be reassigned as necessary to produce the products and models demanded. Such labor flexibility also provides limited protection against worker layoffs. That is, when total demand is down or higher productivity reduces the number of workers needed, they may be reassigned rather than laid off. But sooner or later, if demand keeps dropping, layoffs are necessary. Kawasaki, Lincoln, experienced a full range of such courses of action in 1981–1982.

98

Reassignments

The first overstaffing problems surfaced in spring 1981. JIT-in-duced productivity improvements were reducing needs for direct labor faster than management had projected. Normal attrition was supposed to have taken care of the excess labor, but it did not. The surplus grew—10, 20, then 30 or more employees. The first stage of worker reassignments were from direct labor to essential support tasks such as modifying, installing, and moving equipment. The next stage was assignment of excess employees to maintenance work such as painting, caulking, and minor re-modeling. In June, a touring delegation from the Repetitive Man-ufacturing Group of the American Production and Inventory Control Society were startled to see five Kawasaki employees stuffing crepe paper into a chicken-wire frame to make a float for a parade.

Later in the year the labor surplus problem was compounded by the deepening recession, which was hard on the motorcycle industry and stopped the snowmobile industry virtually dead in its tracks. (Kawasaki permanently closed down its snowmobile product line late in the year.) In October Kawasaki took the per-haps unprecedented step of lending 11 of its excess employees to the City of Lincoln. They worked for the city for several months, with Kawasaki paying regular wages and benefits.

Layoffs

Later in October the first layoffs occurred, as 24 white-collar people were asked to leave. In November, 16 blue-collar workers voluntarily resigned in return for a large severance bonus, and half a dozen more voluntarily agreed to a six-month layoff with call-back rights.

Nonvoluntary terminations finally were put into force in

February 1982. Ninety-eight production workers were terminated as the recessionary slump deepened. Some employees were bitter, because they perceived some of the layoffs as being attributable to the productivity gains generated by just-in-time system improvements—which all employees had been involved in.

Layoffs, Pro and Con

The news media have told us all about the Japanese lifetime employment/no layoff system (applicable especially to full-time male employees in larger companies). Perhaps we expect something of the same sort from Japanese-owned subsidiaries outside of Japan. Actually, Japanese executives seem to relish operating in a country in which they are free to lay off people for good reason. That viewpoint surfaced in an interview, sponsored by *Fortune* magazine, of four executives of Japanese subsidiaries in the United States (Sony, YKK, Kikkoman, and Sanyo).[8]

However, Kawasaki went to some lengths to avoid layoffs here, and most other Japanese companies are probably similarly inclined. But seeing that their American employees will quit the company if they feel like it is some justification for a company to feel it has the right to lay off American employees when necessary. Tit for tat.

Actually, at one time there was a plan at Kawasaki to avoid layoffs or cushion the blow through establishment of a special fund.[9] Early in 1981 the American plant manager and personnel manager had devised a "labor reserve," a formal entry in the company's balance sheet. Monthly transfusions of funds were placed in the labor reserve account by the company. The intention was to use the fund rather like supplemental unemployment benefits for employees on temporary layoffs. Other possible uses included money for retraining, severance bonuses to "buy" voluntary resignations, and funds for establishment of job-referral services. But in October 1981, in a major reorganization of Kawasaki, U.S.A., the marketing division was sold off as a separate entity. In the process, either through partial oversight or deliberate action by corporate headquarters in Japan, the labor reserve account was absorbed and dissolved.

One might conclude from the Kawasaki experience that it is best not to engage extensively in just-in-time project activities during a recession if you can help it, because the JIT-induced productivity gains will exacerbate the excess labor and layoff problem. But there is a strong counterargument that Kawasaki was quite correct in proceeding with JIT improvements under full steam right through the recession. Part of the counterargument is that a recession is when everybody has *time* to rethink and tinker with the production system. More importantly, when motorcycle demand picks up, Kawasaki will enjoy a significant productivity advantage (relative to before the recession), which in the longer run is the soundest way to provide job security to its employees.

Techniques and Behaviors

This chapter tells about techniques that Kawasaki, Lincoln, has successfully implemented. It also tells a bit about the way in which managers made decisions, the role of staff, and the reactions of line supervisors and workers. The intended message of the chapter concerns the *relationship between* the techniques and the behaviors of the people involved. As more just-in-time techniques were implemented at Kawasaki, the American personnel in the plant shed more of their American bad habits. Managers and staff became less inclined to go off on tangents, promote pet projects, further their own interests, and feather their own nests. Each just-in-time improvement thrust people's fortunes closer together, thus shutting out divisive behaviors that the Americans may have brought with them when they hired on.

101

To close this chapter along these same lines, the following restatement of the fourth lesson is offered:

The Kawasaki, Nebraska, experience is that Western managers and workers behave more like their Japanese counterparts as just-in-time techniques are adopted.

CHAPTER 5

Plant Configurations

LESSON 5: Simplify, and goods will flow like water.

A point made in Chapter 1 is that the Japanese have become the world's experts in repetitive manufacturing. That is hard for Americans to get used to. Those of us who are old enough recall the awesome mass-production of war materials during World War II. In the affluent years since that war, the same industrial machine has cranked out equally awesome quantities of consumer goods—which spill out of our houses into mini-warehouses and eventually end up as garbage bulldozed into sanitary landfills to form newly usable real estate. Sure, we know that a good share of it now comes from Japan. But we still like to identify U.S. manufacturing with the production line, repetitively making masses of identical consumer goods. (Each semester I arrange for plant tours with a few local plants, and each of my students may pick one of the plants to tour. The popular tours are to plants known to have assembly lines. I get the impression that

103

the other types of plants—the vast majority—are somehow thought to be illegitimate examples of manufacturing.)

The production-line image is a good one to hold. It is the image that the Kawasaki plant manager, Dennis Butt, had when he stated, "I envision the entire plant as a series of stations on the assembly line, whether physically there or not." Butt, of course, was expressing his vision of how his American plant should be configured in order to accommodate just-in-time production and match the productivity achieved by Kawasaki plants in Japan.

Ultimate Plant Configuration

Assembly lines are not the ultimate in efficiency. Assembly lines are generally labor-intensive, and the human beings doing the assembling are subject to human inconsistencies. The lines cough and sputter and sometimes even have a few inventory buffers between selected stages along the line. The ultimate is not assembly-line production but continuous production, which is found in what are often known as process industries. Lotless production is possible in process industries, such as refining, because it is in the nature of many of the products—liquids, gases, flakes, pellets —to flow continuously rather than to be apportioned into lots; also, process industries are highly automated (capital-intensive), which avoids human inconsistencies and the need for buffer inventories.

The Japanese have built some impressive continous-process factories. For example, foreign steelmakers are in awe of Nippon Kokan's highly automated steel plant built on Ohgishima island in Tokyo Bay. The island was virtually rebuilt. Then over $3.5 billion was invested in plant construction. The plant employs an extensive network of computers and automated material handling; continuous casting of steel slabs and blooms; recycling, recovery, and reuse of everything from water to heat to dust; and the most effective pollution control system among the world's steel plants. And the small number of workers in this highly automated plant is particularly impressive to visiting steelmakers.

In the steel industry and in aluminum, petrochemicals, glass, and other process industries, capital investment is surely the key to high productivity. Management systems seem less important because the highly automated processes physically incorporate controls over volume, quality, and cost—and employ little labor, thereby minimizing problems stemming from worker inconsistency.

In this book we focus on industries in which the management itself is critical, and that encompasses just about all manufacturing other than the process industries. While the products of the process industries flow and may be counted in fractional parts (gallons, tons, linear feet, etc.), the products of the nonprocess industries are counted in whole units (or, as we say in academia, *discrete* units, as opposed to continuous output). Whole units have individualistic properties:

1. They can be made, inspected, stored, and counted out one at a time, or ten at a time, or in batches of any other size.

2. While in process, individual units can form queues and jostle, or be jostled, for priority like shoppers at a supermarket.

3. And, according to Western production management thought, legions of planners and controllers may be needed to help the units through the often complex, multistage manufacturing process.

It is the third point that is called into question in this book, because the Japanese have developed simpler management approaches. The Japanese just-in-time system simplifies by making unit processing as much like continuous processing as possible.

105

In industries that have been able to automate final assembly, such as bottlers and canners, the result is close enough to continuous processing for the label "process industry" to have some justification. For most consumer and industrial goods manufacturing, however, automated assembly lines are still a futuristic dream, and automating subassembly and parts fabrication is even more remote. There are several stages of plant configuration improvements to go through over a span of many years before getting to highly automated plants.

In the remainder of the chapter, we shall examine five stages of configuration that the various shops in a plant may pass through in moving toward repetitive operations and full JIT production.

The five configurations, or stages of physical plant development, are:

- Job-shop fabrication.

- Dedicated production lines.

- Physically merged production processes.

- Mixed-model processing.

- Automated production lines.[1]

The five configurations are presented with reference to motorcycle manufacturing: cutting and forming frame parts, welding frames, painting frames, subassembling differentials and mounted tires, and assembling motorcycles. Each configuration could, as well, apply to other aspects of motorcycle manufacturing or to many other industries. Each successive configuration is more streamlined physically: in equipment, in layout or arrangement, and in handling aids. "Shop paper" involved in order control is also progressively simplified or streamlined as configurations become more advanced.

In most JIT firms, different areas of the plant will be differently configured, but each area will be evolving toward the more streamlined configurations. In this evolution, configuration stages may be skipped. And all the better if it can be done, because JIT benefits are attained that much more quickly.

Job-Shop Fabrication

Job shop is a standard industrial term that refers to a type of production and plant configuration that is at the opposite extreme from just-in-time. Equipment is arranged by process: for example, all the milling machines together, all the lathes together, all the punch presses together, and so forth. Such an arrangement (referred to as a process layout) is not conducive to JIT production for various reasons, including:

1. An order for a given component part usually involves operations on several different machine tools, and the distances from one machine-tool area to another are too far for quick one-piece-at-a-time parts movements.

2. The equipment and tooling in a job shop are usually general-purpose. That is, they can be set up to make almost anything of a particular type. For example, a foundry can make castings of about any shape, and a lathe can trim or form many types of castings or raw metal into more finished pieces. But the time to set up for a particular job on a general-purpose machine tool or in a foundry can take hours or even days. As was demonstrated in Chapter 2, when setup times and costs are high, it makes economic sense to run large lots.

Frame Welding

The job-shop configuration is shown in Figure 5–1 for the example of motorcycle frame welding. Several general-purpose welding booths draw upon jigs from a central jig-storage area. (A jig is a holding device into which frame parts are clamped for welding.)

107

Figure 5–1. Welding Booths: Job-Shop Configuration

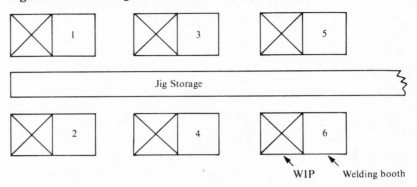

Notes:

    1. WIP: Several days' supply at each booth
    2. Lead time: Several days
    3. Shop paper for every booth:
        A. Job orders
        B. Dispatch List
        C. Move tags

Setting up the jig in a booth for a given job order may take several hours, including first-piece inspection by quality control. An order for a given frame model passes from booth to booth, with more tubing welded into place at each booth.

    Some key characteristics of the job-shop configuration are listed below Figure 5–1. Work-in-process (WIP) inventory waiting to be run at each booth is likely to be several days' supply. Lead time—the time to complete a job order for a particular frame model—is likely to be several days. And in the job shop, heavy-handed production control to cope with the high inventories, jobs in queue, and late orders is normal. Some of the common types of shop paper used by production control are listed in the figure: job orders, daily dispatch lists, and move tags.

Forming Frame Parts from Tubing

From a JIT perspective, the best thing to do with a job shop is to transform it into a production line, which is often a tall order. The next best improvement is to make reductions in setup time so that lot sizes may be economically cut.

One example of this, briefly mentioned in Chapter 2, is the Kawasaki punch presses equipped with roller conveyors to hold dies for quick changeover. Figure 5–2 shows two photographs of one of the presses. The photos show a Bliss 60-ton punch press with a roller conveyor mounted at bed height around the frame like a carousel. About 13 presses are so equipped. Kawasaki's own welders performed the conversions in slack time periods using commonly available roller conveyors, so the cost of conversion was low.

By design or luck—I'm not sure which—all of the punch presses were the same make (Bliss), so that one general blueprint for conversion could be used. In the United States, our imperative to search for the lowest bid often results in a collection of different makes of equipment, which increases costs of stocking repair parts, of maintenance, and of conversion. Japanese plants are far more likely to have the same make for all equipment of a given type.

A punch-press operator at Kawasaki explained her daily routine in forming motorcycle frame parts from lengths of tube stock. Each day's schedule calls for 14 different setups. So each morning she lines up 14 dies on the carousel conveyor and others spilling over to a nearby rack. The dies are arranged in the order of the 14 different parts to be made that day, as specified in the scheduling document. Setup for each new part number entails rolling the die under the chuck and clamping it into place. A number of vertical and horizontal controls are properly adjusted, and the setup may be checked with simple gauging devices. The operator said that it took her about 30 days to become efficient at the daily setup routine. The setup time averages eight to nine minutes, and the total setup time per day for the 14 different part numbers is about three hours.

Before the presses were modified for quick setup, *each* setup took more than three hours. Frequently a setup took closer to a

Figure 5–2. Punch Press Equipped for Quick Die Change

whole day, including time to obtain a lifting device to move a heavy die, time to adjust the bed (now fixed for all dies), and time to chunk out a few parts, have them checked, change settings, try again, and so forth. Once a long setup like that was completed, it

110

made sense to run a few days' worth of the given part number.*
Today, instead of days' worth of one part number, 14 different
part numbers may be run in one day.

Dedicated Production Lines

Sometimes it is feasible to break up the job shop, or part of it, and
rearrange the work centers into a few production lines. Each
production line is dedicated to the manufacture of a different part
number or model or group of similar part numbers. Three modes
of operating dedicated lines are discussed below.

Overlapped Production

If there are a few part numbers made repetitively, each dedicated
line may be "permanently" configured to run just one part number, one piece at a time from station to station. If there are quite
a few part numbers, each made only occasionally, each line may
be dedicated to a few similar part numbers instead of just one. In
that case, there may be some changeover time from one part
number to the next, leading to lots instead of single pieces being
passed from work station to work station.

To cut down the lot-size inventories in process, the concept
of *overlapped production* may be employed. Suppose, for example, that you start 50 of widget model *A* every morning and 50 of
widget model *B* every afternoon. If a full lot of 50 *A*'s gets passed
from work center to work center down the dedicated production
line, followed by 50 *B*'s, then the average inventory at each station is 50 units—hardly a just-in-time operation. To gain JIT ben-

---

* Manufacturing people tend to use the term "part number" instead of
"part" to avoid confusion; i.e., you know that the plural of "part number"
refers to more than one *different* part, whereas you are not sure about the
meaning of "parts."

efits, it becomes desirable to overlap the production of a lot among the several work stations. That is, one station may make a few of *A* (1 or 2 or 5 perhaps), which are delivered to the next station, then make a few more and deliver them, and so on until the whole lot of 50 has been produced. Then all the work stations convert to run model B. The lot of 50 is strung out over several stations so that idle inventory at each station is negligible.

The concept of overlapped production is well known among Western job-shop managers. However, it is thought of as an expediting tool. That is, when a parts order is running behind schedule, a production controller may expedite by having a portion of the order moved ahead while another portion is still being worked on in the first work center. In more formal job-shop control systems, special written instructions may need to be issued to inform the work center supervisors and parts movement people about this expediting action.

In Japanese industry, overlapped production has come to be recognized as one more way to move toward JIT, and not just an expediting action.

The Daily Schedule

When the volume of a given part number justifies dedicating the production line to that one part number alone, piece-for-piece processing becomes feasible. Idle in-process inventory disappears completely. Furthermore, cumbersome order-tracking aids —job orders, dispatch lists, move tags—that production control uses in the job-shop mode may be done away with. Documentation may be reduced to a daily schedule for each line.

Kawasaki, Lincoln, implemented this configuration in frame welding in spring 1981. The job-shop configuration shown in Figure 5–1 was replaced by the dedicated-line configuration shown in Figure 5–3. The welders built the lines themselves in slack time periods. There are about six lines, each equipped with the proper

112

Figure 5–3. Dedicated Welding Lines (Group Technology)

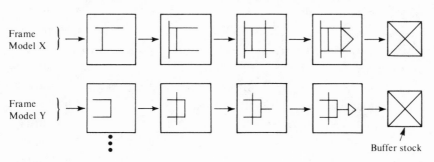

Notes:
1. Lead Time: 1-4 hours
2. *Without* kanban:
   A. Completed frames: 1-2 days' (maximum) buffer stock
   B. Shop paper for each line: a daily schedule
3. *With* kanban:
   A. Completed frames: fill a few standard containers
   B. One kanban per empty container (from the next work center, frame painting)

welding jigs for a different size of motorcycle frame. As the figure suggests, for the two sample lines—frame models X and Y—two or three pieces of tubing may be placed in a jig for welding at station 1; passed to station 2, where more pieces are welded in place using another jig; and so on. The line must be carefully balanced in order to provide the welders with roughly equal amounts of work. Balance may be achieved by timing the amount of welding done at each station and adding or subtracting the number of welds to be made at a given station, as necessary. Jig design must, of course, match the number of pieces to be welded at a given station.

Not shown in Figure 5–3 are stocks of cut tube pieces, which would be stationed at each booth. The tube inventory is the responsibility of the preceding punch-press shop where the tube pieces are made. The only idle inventory that frame welding is responsible for is the completed frame stock, designated by the square with the x inside, at the ends of the lines. This is buffer stock. If the rate of welding output were completely predictable and invariable, that buffer stock could be wiped out, but, of

113

course, the inconsistencies of the human welders make that unlikely or impossible.

Key characteristics of the dedicated production line configuration are listed in Figure 5–3. Point 1: Lead time to complete a frame used to be several days in the job-shop configuration; now it is 1 to 4 hours. Point 2, designated "without kanban," applies to this discussion. The buffer stock has been cut from several days' supply *at every welding booth* in the job-shop configuration to a one- or two-day supply of completed frames at the end of each line. Shop paper now consists simply of a daily schedule. Point 3 applies to the following discussion.

Forward Linkage by Means of Kanban

With the same physical configuration—dedicated production lines—a further step toward just-in-time production may be attained by use of kanban instead of a daily schedule. Kawasaki has not taken this step in frame welding (but *has* done so in final assembly—explained in a later chapter). One reason is that for frame painting, the next process after frame welding, considerable work is needed to upgrade the painting center's present configuration. When that happens, the painting center could communicate a need for more welded frames by the kanban system: Cards (kanban) attached to empty racks (point 3 in Figure 5–3) for holding frames would be sent back to the frame-welding center to signal the need to produce more of a certain frame model. The number of cards/racks serves as the buffer stock and is set to correspond with the variability of the welding line's production rate.

As we know from Chapter 2, the kanban system features deliberate management action to remove buffer inventory in order to expose the workers to the consequences and motivate correction of the irregularities causing the problem. In the case of the welding lines, the management action would be to remove

114

frame racks with kanban attached. Such difficulties as cantankerous clamping devices on welding jigs or a defective welding torch might be exposed as problems needing correction.

A characteristic of kanban is that if the using work center should have a breakdown, the supplying work center ceases to receive kanban and therefore can run low, or out, of work to do. In the welding/painting example, if painting ceases, then the welding center will soon run out of kanban order cards and empty racks. The usual Western response would be to keep on welding anyway, in order not to idle the welders and their facilities. The Japanese response is to stop welding. It is a fundamental JIT principle: *Do not make parts that are unneeded simply to keep busy.* Kawasaki managers take some delight in claiming to outside visitors that they adhere to this principle. What would they do with the idle welders? Put them to work on maintenance, send them out to the assembly line, or, if worse comes to worst, send them home.

Physical Merger of Processes

The third-stage configuration is physical merger of processes. The advantages are elimination of inventory buffers and shop paper as well, resulting in a highly simplified and streamlined operation. There are at least two ways to accomplish physical merger of processes. One is simply to position the end of the feeder process adjacent to the point of use. The second way, known as *group technology* (GT), consists of breaking up two or more processes and recombining them into cells, each capable of performing the whole enlarged task. Much of what has been written in English about GT has come out of Great Britain.[2] But I have found, as others have, that it is the Japanese who extensively implement GT. I have encountered a fascinating example of GT, facilitated by manufacture of "homemade" machine tools, at the Akashi, Japan, factory of Kawasaki Motors.

Group Technology and "Homemade" Machine Tools

For some months before I was able to visit the Akashi motorcycle plant, I had been hearing from friends at Kawasaki, Lincoln, that the plant in Japan had followed the GT concept to physically merge the punch press and welding stages in the production of motorcycle frames. The marriage seemed unlikely to me. I was hard put to imagine how a huge, ungainly, 60-ton press could be combined with welder's apparatus.

What I witnessed in the Akashi plant (which was later scheduled to be implemented in the Lincoln plant) were 6-ton or 8-ton or 10-ton screw presses instead of large punch presses. Kawasaki toolmakers had designed and made the small screw presses specifically for notching and bending tubing into frame parts. Each press is equipped with its own die permanently in place, so that there is *no* setup time, and therefore no requirement for training to set up and run. The *welder* runs the presses, and in a piece-by-piece pure just-in-time mode. The screw presses are slow but sure. The welder may load one press to make one piece he needs, then another press for a second piece, and another for a third piece, and so on. As each piece is finished in the press, the welder may place it in a welding jig and weld it to the growing motorcycle frame. Of course, the steps may be sequenced to minimize delays.

In a typical Western machine shop, skilled machinists run the punch presses, sometimes with the aid of engineers, quality control people, or specially trained setup crews who assure that dies are properly mounted and adjusted. As was discussed earlier in the chapter, Kawasaki, Lincoln, has simplified the process by equipping punch presses with carousel die-handling roller conveyors; unskilled, less highly paid workers can learn to perform the setups in 30 days or so. At Akashi, the small screw presses eliminate press operators as a separate skill altogether. The grouping of several process steps saves on inventories, coordination, paperwork, and supervision, and the welder now has control over almost all the elements of quality related to the frames.

This example nicely illustrates the tandem application of group technology and internally produced machine tools to transform separate processes into an integrated just-in-time operation, with resultant productivity and quality benefits. All that I had heard and seen previously concerning GT and homemade machine tools in Japanese industry had been indicative of separate treatment of these concepts. The innovation at Akashi is one more example of the integrativeness of the production-management approaches that have evolved in Japan.

Adjacency

Figure 5–4 illustrates the alternative to GT in achieving physical merger of processes. In the figure, dedicated frame welding lines merge with frame painting, which merges with the motorcycle assembly line. Shop paper, even kanban, is eliminated. The rate of frame painting and frame welding is simply matched to the rate of motorcycle assembly. Inventory buffers are entirely elimi-

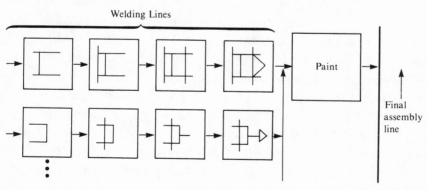

Notes:
1. Shop paper for welding and paint: none

Figure 5–4. Dedicated Lines, Physically Linked Forward

117

nated within the long production line. But, of course, there are still feeder stocks of external inventories: cut tubing and welding supplies in the welding center, paint in the painting center, and a variety of other parts and small hardware in final assembly.

The Kawasaki, Lincoln, plant is probably years away from physical merger of frame welding, painting, and final assembly. However, physical merger of processes has been achieved in other areas. Two such mergers occurred in 1981 in connection with the JIT program.

The first example is the physical merger of differential sub-assembly with final assembly of Kawasaki's three-wheeled rec-reational bike (the "KLT"). The differentials had been sub-assembled in lots off-line. But the foremen of the KLT line, perhaps responding to the challenge implied in the plant manag-er's plant vision, led a project to move the differential line so that completed differentials physically merge with final KLT assem-bly at the using assembly-line station. Now the inventory is gen-erally only one or two completed differentials, as opposed to a whole rack or pallet load when they were subassembled in lots out of sight of the using station on the assembly line. The fore-man's own KLT assemblers did the work of moving the subas-sembly facilities in slack time periods.

(A side remark is in order here: This is the third time that I've mentioned doing other work "in slack time periods." Is slack time a symptom of problems? No. A JIT plant is likely to generate slack time (1) because of the principle of not making unneeded parts just to keep busy, and (2) because of the practice of deliberately pulling workers off the line—freeing them for "slack time" tasks—when the line is running smoothly, in order to expose and correct the hidden problems. Also, of course, the total quality control concept of less-than-full-capacity scheduling builds in slack for the sake of avoiding haste-induced quality problems.)

The second example concerns the subassembly area where tires were mounted onto wheels. As was explained in Chapter 4,

118

the mounted tires had been transferred to final motorcycle assembly by an overhead conveyor. The new Japanese management team in the fall of 1981 called for abandonment of the conveyor and relocation of tire mounting adjacent to the tire using-station on the final assembly line. Now the inventory of mounted tires is only one or two.

Mixed Models

Figure 5–5 shows the fourth configuration, mixed-model processing. The mixed-model configuration operates with a single production line in place of multiple dedicated lines (or dedicated GT centers). Extensive tooling changes may be required. Probably the retooling would consist mainly of welding-fixture redesign to make the fixtures flexible enough to hold cut tubing properly for any model of motorcycle frame. Kawasaki has not attempted this, and it may be impractical to try to design such fixtures. But the *concept* of running mixed models is not unusual at all. Our farm-implement companies have years of experience assembling farm tractors on mixed-model assembly lines.

As was mentioned earlier, mixed-model *assembly* lines may

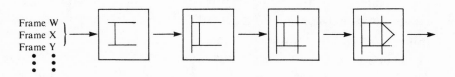

Notes:
1. Single line simplifies JIT linkages with upstream
   and downstream processes
2. Shop paper options:
   A. Daily schedule
   B. Kanban
   C. None; physical link with next process

Figure 5–5. Single Line Running Mixed Models

not be difficult to achieve, because assembly tends to be labor-intensive and labor is flexible. To perform an assembly operation on a different model may simply require grabbing a different part and a different hand tool. *Subassembly* is generally more capital-intensive, and the equipment—or capital, as the economists call it (e.g., welding jigs)—is not so inherently flexible. *Fabrication* is still more capital-intensive, requiring, for example, machine tools such as punch presses, milling machines, and injection molding machines. In the United States we have generally rejected the very notion of running mixed models in subassembly and fabrication. But the Japanese try hard to do so. Kawasaki's carousel conveyor-equipped punch presses are an example of attempts to move toward mixed-model processing even in fabrication.

Line balancing is a special challenge in mixed-model operations, because different models may have different work contents. For example, a large model may take more minutes of labor time or machine time than a small model. The line would have to run at the speed of the slowest model, which means some idle time at every station when the small model is passing through. Line-balancing options are to run two small models for every large one, or three small ones for every two large ones, and so forth.

Line balancing is a fairly well developed part of Western industrial management technology. Unfortunately, much of what the Japanese do deviates sharply from classical Western line-balancing principles and concepts. The issue is treated in a separate chapter later in the book.

The mixed-model, single-line configuration sharply reduces the number of stations, amount of equipment, and required floor space—as compared with multiple dedicated lines. Inventory is reduced because there is buffer stock at the end of only one mixed-model line rather than buffers at the end of several dedicated lines. Furthermore, it is easier for the downstream process (e.g., painting) to communicate or physically interact with a single line, an advantage that makes it easier to introduce kanban or physically merge the processes. A single line also simplifies inter-

120

action with preceding work centers and may cut buffer stocks of parts coming from those work centers. And there also may be less need for supervision and shop floor control, since workers stay put at a single line. By contrast, with multiple dedicated lines it is common for workers to be moved from line to line during the day to make different models.

Bill Harahan, director of manufacturing planning at Ford Motor Co., has data closely comparing a Japanese plant layout with a North American plant layout for the *same product*. The product is an automotive power train on which both the Japanese and North American companies had prepared bids. The Japanese company's bid called for a plant investment of $100 million, as compared with $300 million for the North American company. Equipment requirements were about the same: 41 machines if the Japanese plant got the contract; 39 machines if the North American plant did the work. But the proposed plant layout for the North American plant called for 900,000 square feet to hold 39 machines, as opposed to only 300,000 square feet to hold the 41 machines proposed in the Japanese plant layout!

Harahan explains the difference as follows (this account is based on transcripts of a speech given a number of times to executives of various supplier companies of Ford):

> The basic difference is all the white space you see in the Ford schematic . . . which is used for in-process storage, and you would immediately raise the question, well with no in-process storage, if one machine goes down the line goes down. That is exactly the case. That is the drill with the Japanese. They have no in-process storage. . . . In their view, if there is a problem and the machine goes down and the line goes down, they fix it. Now that requires an extraordinarily rigid system of preventive maintenance, which they put in place.

Harahan also showed slides demonstrating further differences between the bids: the "virtual absence of material-handling devices" and use of simpler, cheaper machines in the Japanese plant.

Harahan's data illustrate several Japanese production concepts: extremely tight inventory control, which was fully explained in Chapter 2; very low investment in material-handling equipment, which was covered in Chapter 4 (see "Conveyor Removal"); and rigorous preventive maintenance, plus use of inexpensive machines, which were commented on in earlier chapters and will be more fully explained in Chapter 6. But Harahan was demonstrating these concepts in terms of plant configuration: The Japanese plant layout provides *no space* for inventory, so there is no room to store large lots of parts that might tumble out of a large U.S.-style "super machine," and no need for a lot of material-handling gear since there is little inventory to handle. The Japanese ideal is: Make a piece, check it, and hand it to the next worker; the next worker's machine is close by and there is no place to put parts except at that next worker's station. The Western approach is: Make a bunch of parts on a fast machine, set them down somewhere, and periodically call for a forklift truck to move batches between work stations—or use conveyors.

Automated Production Lines

According to *Webster's New World Dictionary,* the word "automation" was coined in about 1949—not that many years ago. It is no wonder that extensive examples of it are hard to find (except, as has been explained, in the process industries: glass, steel, paper, plastics, petroleum, etc.). Contrary to what the news media would have us believe, even the Japanese have scarcely begun the enormous task of automating their durable-goods manufacturing plants. The claim that the Japanese had installed 75,000 robots was appearing in news reports in 1979 and 1980. But Kanji Yonemoto, executive director of the Japan Industrial Robot Association, says that 61,000 of these are either inflexible pick-and-place devices or what the Japanese call "manual manipulators,'' requiring human operation.[3] American engineers prefer to think of true robots as fully automatic and programmable, i.e., capable of changing their motion patterns simply by being fed a different program.

Pseudo-Robots

But pick-and-place devices and manual manipulators—pseudo-robots—are not to be sneered at. In a JIT-oriented factory it is natural to look upon such devices as advanced means of further reducing buffer inventories, thus triggering another round of JIT benefits.

Management action is the catalyst: As we have seen, when everyone along a production line is keeping up with the flow rate, management removes buffer inventories or workers, with the result that certain workers begin to have trouble keeping up without causing defectives. Problem points are exposed, and everyone looks for ways to solve the problem. Figure 5–6 highlights the portion of the JIT model dealing with problem awareness and solutions.

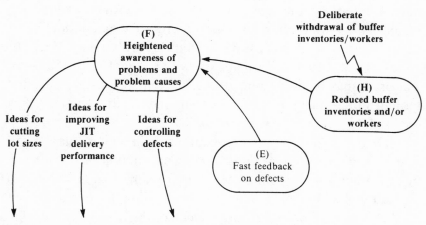

Figure 5–6. JIT Production: Problem Awareness and Solutions

Sooner or later the pseudo-robot option will be attractive, as compared with further improvements of hand tools, controls, parts feeder devices, and fixtures; preventive maintenance; and other such simple solutions. That is, when you have provided all possible efficiency-improving aids and the worker still has problems keeping up, you begin automating the worker's tasks. Hard-to-do, dangerous, or monotonous tasks are likely candidates for automation, and the pick-and-place devices and manual manipulators are often the obvious and least costly way to automate. They often can work faster and nearly always can work more steadily and with fewer mistakes—which solves problems exposed when buffer inventory or workers are removed. It is becoming common to see, in advanced JIT factories in Japan, a mixture of human beings and simple or pseudo robots along production lines. Of course, the ratio of devices to people increases over time.

Robots

While pick-and-place devices and manual manipulators can improve JIT performance on a production line, they lack the flexibility to change from one model to another. And as we know, mixed-model production lines are superior to single-model lines. Pure robots have the necessary flexibility. A robot may "feel" or "see" or "be told" automatically what model is at the work station. It may be programmed to adjust dimensions, speeds, and tooling and to reach for different component parts when a different model is there to be worked on.

There are a few existing examples—in Japan, the United States, and some other countries—of production processes run mostly or entirely by robots. Most such examples appear to be in the automobile industry: in auto body welding, for example. But the Japanese will probably forge ahead of the rest of the world in robot applications in the next few years. One reason is that Japanese JIT production management exposes productivity bottle-necks and marshals line and staff engineering talent to relieve the bottlenecks; some of the time, the solutions will be robots.

Furthermore, Japan *needs* robots because of high labor costs, coupled with a growing labor shortage. The labor shortage is attributable to a low birthrate, which began to drop about 1950 and is still falling. Whereas the postwar baby boom lasted some 17 years in the United States, Japan's baby boom lasted only 3 years.[4] Lacking an ample supply of new labor to fuel expansion, Japan has resorted to subsidiary plants overseas and to produc-tivity enhancements at home. Robots are particularly attractive because they ease the labor shortage and are not subject to the seniority-based pay increases that a human work force demands year after year.

The United States, by contrast, has had plenty of new work-ers, whose low entry-level pay holds down the overall average pay rate. Our own large baby-boom population is now in the labor market and will move into higher pay brackets. However, an endless supply of immigrant labor, which seems destined to con-tinue, serves to check the wage-rate growth. As one labor econ-omist put it,[5] the United States may welcome Mexican and Haitian immigrants with open arms later in this decade in order to feed industrial expansion, fill service-sector jobs, and hold down average wage growth.

Computer-aided Design and Manufacturing

While the demographer might conclude that the United States does not need robots, this does not tell the full story. The United States is still the industrial giant of the world and is still the leader in productivity per employee. To stay that way, robots are needed. And a rosy robot future seems likely because of U.S. dominance in computers. No other country is even close to ours in development of computer-aided design (CAD) and computer-aided manufacturing (CAM). In the CAD/CAM factory of the future (some prototypes already exist) a product designer at a CAD terminal designs the product on the screen; CAM computer software automatically translates the product design into orders for component parts; and microcomputer-controlled robots automatically make, move, and assemble the customer order. The computers may be linked together and may tie in with business analysis software. Then a customer order may be computer-simulated even before the order is accepted, so that profitability and proper pricing may be accurately determined in advance.

CAD/CAM planning, with robot-based operations, constitutes an advanced form of JIT/TQC production. CAD and CAM compress planning lead times so that the factory may make the product very soon—"just in time"—after the customer asks for it; and robots can quickly make products of consistently good quality without waste, rework, buffer stocks, and so forth, thus compressing manufacturing lead time.

The cost of CAD/CAM/robot factories is, of course, enormous. It will take many years before such technology has a significant impact (except in selected industries). I prefer that this book be about the present and the next five or ten years. Therefore, let us return to issues that are more current.

Conveyors and Stacker Cranes

I worked for about two years as a materials-handling (MH) engineer. I took a materials-handling course offered by a top consultant, attended MH trade fairs, subscribed to the MH trade magazines, and coordinated plant MH projects. I learned that the sexy MH devices in the United States were the computer-controlled conveyors and stacker cranes. A stacker crane can be installed in the center of a plant surrounded by storage racks as much as 40 feet high. Manufactured lots of component parts and subassemblies may be placed in tote boxes on a conveyor, which automatically moves the tote boxes to the stacker crane. The stacker crane, a self-propelled, computer-controlled vehicle resembling a very tall forklift, picks the tote box off the conveyor and moves it horizontally and vertically to an empty pigeonhole somewhere among the storage racks. The tote box is left there, and its location and other identifying data are retained in computer memory. On some other day, when parts are needed for an end-product order, the parts are retrieved by a reverse process.

The underlying assumption pertaining to stacker cranes, conveyors, and other such devices is that parts will be made or bought in large lots and therefore *need* to be stored and retrieved. That assumption is, of course, in opposition to the JIT production concept. It is no wonder that, as was stated earlier, the Japanese now view conveyors as undesirable in connection with manned work stations—or, at best, a necessary evil.

Automatic Quality Monitoring

One final type of automation, automatic quality monitoring, was explained in the Chapter 3 discussion of "foolproof" devices, or *bakayoke*—which warrant brief further comment here. In the industrialized West automatic quality monitoring devices are common enough in the process industries, but relatively rare in goods-manufacturing industries. The Japanese subsidiary plants in the West are gradually introducing such devices. But the rationale for their introduction really is not there in typical Western plants that produce in large lots. Use of automatic quality checking encourages smaller lots—movement toward JIT processing —and vice versa.

Plant Configurations and Market Positioning

In my scheme for classifying plant configurations, the job shop is valued least, and each higher-level configuration receives pro-

127

gressively more praise. In all fairness, the very best manufacturing companies—the Toyotas and Sonys of the world—nearly always begin as job shops. And many of the world's most talented industrial workers are in job shops: highly skilled machinists, welders, tool and die makers, and so forth. In fact, a job shop is a job shop partly because of the skill levels of its workers. These persons in the skilled trades can read blueprints and set up their own complex machinery to make whatever is called for, often without much need for engineering and supervisory assistance. Their firms sell this skill at a high price. Thus, the job shop serves a need and extracts commensurate profits. It has its market niche.

But the greatest rewards lie in growth. With few exceptions, job-shop owners want to evolve into industrial giants. The message that seems clear from the Japanese experience is that job shops should not grow into bigger job shops. They should invest early in streamlined configurations.

Johnson Gear

A local company in Lincoln, Nebraska, comes to mind: Johnson Gear Division of Arrow Gear Corp., a manufacturer of right-angle gears, which attach to irrigation pumps and other devices. Johnson Gear's market position is based on fast response to customer orders. Its modest-sized plant in Lincoln employs about 50 workers, including skilled machinists and assemblers. There are only 11 different product models (with a variety of options), and sales have been growing rapidly every year.

Conditions seem right for Johnson Gear to evolve to a streamlined repetitive mode of production, and the company already knows how to do it. In early 1981, orders poured in. Castings, bought from outside foundries, bypassed the storeroom; they were moved into the machine shop as fast as they arrived on the loading docks—the kind of dock-to-line receiving that is the everyday norm in JIT plants such as Kawasaki. In the machine shop, the bottleneck operation was drilling; the flow through the drill work center needed to be speeded up. Special rails were rigged up between two of the multiple-spindle drills, and lots were overlapped—run piece by piece—between the two machines; the rails served to move the heavy castings quickly and without the need for much vertical or horizontal alignment. By these and other measures, throughput time was cut and output greatly increased. "We were really cooking," was the way one employee put it.

In the next few months demand fell way off. The production-line mode of machining was halted, and the plant returned to normal. Purchased castings and other parts go into storage and later out to the shop floor for machining; machined parts are made in lots and go back to storage until needed in final assembly, whose production corresponds strictly to customer orders. This mode of operations requires a very large storeroom: 15,000 square feet of warehouse out of the 45,000-square-foot building. More work-in-process inventory is out on the shop floor.

Responding to Growth

If Johnson Gear follows the usual U.S. pattern of coping with growth, the storerooms will continue to increase and computer-based production control, including MRP, will probably be developed to keep all the orders and inventories straight. The small, simple job shop will become a large, complex job shop.

Could Johnson Gear adopt JIT instead? The plant configuration changes are no obstacle. The company already has some experience at streamlining the production flow. At the input end, purchasing, changes would have to be made. Currently Johnson Gear buys castings and bearings from producers all over the country. In Japanese JIT purchasing, a given item is bought from only one or two nearby suppliers and the same suppliers are kept "forever." The benefits of this type of buying are too extensive to discuss here, but are examined in a later chapter.

The other JIT issue is at the output end: Could Johnson Gear provide four-week deliveries to customers, as it does now, without a substantial inventory of parts ready to be slapped together, painted, and shipped? I believe so. The JIT-induced inventory reductions would be gradual, depending upon how long it took to reconfigure the various work centers in the plant and to cement stable JIT purchasing agreements with local-area suppliers. But the delivery response time would be expected to hold firm—while the JIT system would yield improved quality and productivity, which would further stimulate growth.

The Johnson Gear example presents some of the issues involved in converting to JIT from the job-shop configuration, which is the dominant configuration among producers of discrete goods in Western industry. In the next chapter issues related to more advanced JIT configurations are examined—specifically the question of balancing JIT production lines.

Lakes and Rivers

In this chapter I have tried to paint two pictures. One is a picture of a plant made up of job shops, separate from each other like the lakes that dot a map of Minnesota. The other is a picture of a plant configured as a streamlined collection of closely linked processes. The system of streams and rivers forming the mighty Amazon Basin comes to mind; the current is capable of carrying along a variety of materials. We need such pictures. We need to have concrete visualizations of what we are striving for, not just abstract terms like "efficiency," "lot size," and "robot."

The central point of the chapter may be expressed, in conclusion, as a restatement of the fifth lesson:

Emphasize simpler plant configurations—break down the barriers between shops.

130

CHAPTER 6

Production-Line Management

LESSON 6: Flexibility opens doors.

As we have seen, productivity, quality, and worker motivation are benefits of repetitive production line operations. Production lines make units one at a time, generally with no inventory buffers between successive operations—the pure just-in-time mode of production. Ideally, mixed models may be run so that the production-line schedule closely matches market demand.

Production lines are certainly not a Japanese innovation. Production-line manufacturing, popularly known as mass production, had its roots in the industrial revolution of Europe and the United States. (Implementation, circa 1800, of Eli Whitney's notion of interchangeable parts was a key enabling event in the development of mass production.) Running mixed models on a single production line also has Western roots. Scholarly articles on the subject have been available for a number of years, although the writings generally refer to assembly lines, implying final as-

131

sembly but not subassembly and fabrication. In this chapter we shall look at some of the striking differences between Western and Japanese design and management of production lines. The basic differences are presented first, followed by some discussion of applications in Japanese foreign subsidiaries, chiefly Kawasaki.

Western vs. Japanese Emphasis

Leading Japanese manufacturers would mostly agree with Western principles of production-line design, as presented, for example, in Wild's thorough book on the subject.[1] Japanese innovations in production-line design do not cast off Western principles but do change the emphasis: To put it simply, the Western emphasis is on good balance, whereas the Japanese place as much or more emphasis on flexibility. Figure 6–1 (discussed below) contrasts the Western and Japanese tendencies.

Top Priority

A production line is said to be in balance when every worker's task takes the same amount of time. Line balancing is a manufacturing-engineering function in which the whole collection of production-line tasks are chopped up into equal portions, with each portion being assigned to a different worker. There are mathematical, procedural, and computer-based approaches to designing well-balanced production lines. These approaches are treated, in English, in scores of journal articles and chapters of books, and even constitute the entire subject matter of a few books. Where production lines are concerned, Western emphasis is clearly centered on the issue of balance, item 1 in Figure 6–1.

Japanese manufacturers also want their lines to balance, for

Figure 6–1. Production Lines: Western vs. Japanese

WESTERN	JAPANESE
1. Top priority: line balance	Top priority: flexibility
2. Strategy: stability—long production runs so that the need to rebalance seldom occurs	Strategy: flexibility—expect to rebalance often to match output to changing demand
3. Assume fixed labor assignments	Flexible labor; move to the problems or to where the current workload is
4. Use inventory buffers to cushion effects of equipment failure	Employ maximal preventive maintenance to keep equipment from breaking down
5. Need sophisticated analysis (e.g., using computers) to evaluate and cull the many options	Need human ingenuity to provide flexibility and ways around bottlenecks
6. Planned by staff	Foreman may lead design effort and will adjust plan as needed
7. Plan to run at fixed rate; send quality problems off line	Slow for quality problems; speed up when quality is right
8. Linear or L-shaped lines	U-shaped or parallel lines
9. Conveyorized material movement is desirable	Put stations close together and avoid conveyors
10. Buy "supermachines" and keep them busy	Make (or buy) small machines; add more copies as needed
11. Applied in labor-intensive final assembly	Applied even to capital-intensive subassembly and fabrication work
12. Run mixed models where labor content is similar from model to model	Strive for mixed-model production, even in subassembly and fabrication

well-balanced lines avoid labor idleness and improve productivity. But for a host of interrelated reasons, the best Japanese manufacturers seem to look for flexibility first and line balance second. Western production lines are unlikely to be very flexible because they are planned "off line" by specialists using cumbersome analyses, because of labor and equipment inflexibility, because of line shape, because of quality and inventory buffer policies, and because of basic strategies—each of which is further

133

discussed below. Japanese strategies require flexibility, and get it, by means of procedures and policies that are rather opposite to Western tendencies.

Strategies

Regarding basic strategy (item 2 in Figure 6–1), the Japanese have a fundamental aversion to inventories. The historical reason is that inventories are wasteful; and the national aversion to inventories grows steadily stronger as Japanese industry increasingly experiences the JIT/TQC benefits discussed in Chapter 2. Without inventories production lines are quite naked; that is, the lines are called upon to react right away whenever part models or output rates are changed—which is frequent in Japanese JIT plants. Consumers are fickle and change their patterns of buying, which changes demands on final assembly lines. And innumerable human and physical sources of delay in any manufacturing stage will, in the absence of buffer inventories, be felt soon in preceding stages, including production lines subassembling or fabricating parts. The Japanese strategy is to make their lines flexible enough to absorb these external and internal irregularities.

Since the Western tendency is to allow inventory buffers, line flexibility is not important. The Western line-balancing strategy, therefore, aims for stability: Design and balance the line with long production runs in mind so that the need to rebalance occurs infrequently.

Labor Assignments

One manifestation of the Western strategy of line stability is the tendency for labor assignments to be fixed; see item 3 in Figure 6–1. The production line may employ a few rovers, who help out where needed, but most line workers are not moved about.

134

By contrast, labor flexiblity is an important feature in the Japanese strategy of line flexibility. When one worker is having problems and experiencing delays, other workers move in to help, partly to avoid being idled themselves. The foremen or leadmen may direct workers to the problem, or the workers may move to the problem on their own when they notice a help light turned on by a fellow worker. A second type of labor flexiblity is related to the management practice of deliberately pulling workers off the line when the line is running too smoothly, e.g., when trouble lights are not going on. As was discussed in Chapter 2, the idea is to try to produce with fewer workers, which will expose problems to be corrected. A third need for labor flexibility is connected with the movement of whole crews from one dedicated line to another as the model mix changes. A fourth need for flexiblity pertains to group technology (GT), in which one worker may handle a variety of tasks in a single work center: e.g., the motorcycle frame welder who also makes the frame parts on screw presses (at Kawasaki's Akashi plant). And finally, flexibility is needed to rebalance lines when there is a changeover from one part to another, which tends to occur often in a Japanese JIT factory.

These benefits of labor flexibility are important enough that many Japanese manufacturers have formal policies or even pay systems that recognize flexibility. At Mitsuboshi Belting Co., a major Japanese manufacturer of V-belts, hoses, and other rubber products, most workers are proficient in at least three jobs and may be moved to a different job any time there is a need. At Matsushita Electric Co.'s refrigerator plants in Japan a six-step wage scale is tied to the number of different jobs mastered: The lowest wage steps, L-1, L-2, and L-3, apply to workers who are learning a single job. Step L-4 is for mastery of a single job; L-5 is for mastery of at least three different jobs; and L-6 is for mastery of at least five different jobs.

The lack of such practices in Western companies is explained by Western industry's emphasis on stability, not flexibility. Some

135

of the Japanese subsidiaries in the United States make labor flex-ibility a condition to which newly hired employees must agree.[2]

Equipment Failure

We have seen that in Japanese plants fellow workers may help out with small irregularities involved in performing tasks; an equipment failure is a more serious matter, with the potential to shut down a production line. To avoid such failures, the Japanese are careful not to overload or otherwise tax their machines' ca-pabilities, and workers are trained to perform a daily regimen of machine checking (simple preventive maintenance) before start-ing up in the morning; see item 4 in Figure 6–1. (Daily machine checking was introduced earlier, in Chapter 3, as a total quality control concept.) Furthermore, when there is a breakdown dur-ing the day, the worker himself may have the capability to fix it. By one report, ''They can fix it and have it back in operation in under 15 minutes, compared with the average American time of two to four hours.''[3] Preventive maintenance (PM) includes the keeping of careful records on each machine's usage, careful anal-ysis to determine PM needs and frequencies, having PM workers sign the machine's PM records whenever maintenance is per-formed, and so forth. Such PM practices are recommended in Western books on the subject, and Japanese companies that I visited were zealously following the recommendations.

The idea of workers checking and doing minor repair work on their own equipment is a Japanese development, not pre-scribed in the textbooks. The daily routine of the Japanese worker may begin with exercises and a chorus of the company song, and then a thorough personal check on the condition of his equipment. The worker may go through a checklist to be sure that the equipment will not fail during the day. Anyone familiar with the activities of military or commercial airline pilots will recog-nize this routine. Aircraft maintenance is extremely thorough,

136

but pilots double-check critical devices, using checklists, before taking off. It is no accident that the entire U.S. passenger airline industry completed two years of crash-free operation in late 1981. The point is that if the airlines can avoid critical breakdowns, so can manufacturers, and the Japanese are doing it.

Not so in Western countries. The presumption is, as Wild puts it, that "all equipment, however well designed and maintained, is liable to failure, such failure often occurring without warning." Wild offers the standard Western prescription for coping with failures: "The existence of a buffer stock after the station which is out of service will ensure that the subsequent stations are not immediately 'starved' of work."[4]

The climate for PM in Japan is probably enhanced by the tendency to avoid three-shift operations, except in more highly automated plants, especially in the process industries (e.g., steel, glass, chemicals). Japanese laws prohibit women from working past 10:00 P.M., and besides that, there are maintenance and engineering advantages in not running late shifts: Equipment is free and available for maintenance people, production engineers, and tooling and setup crews to work on after hours.

The plants of small suppliers usually utilize only the day shift, with maintenance crews on hand before and after the shift. Larger Japanese plants have increasingly adopted a two-shift plan. One fairly popular approach to two-shifting is "4–8–4–8–4," which means two eight-hour production shifts nested between three four-hour shifts in which maintenance and tool changes are performed. (Sometimes the maintenance shifts are three and a half hours instead of four.)

Three shifts have been more normal in North America. The rationale is that losses in efficiency on second and third shifts are more than offset by overall daily capacity and productivity gains. After intensive study of two-shifting in Japan, Ford Motor Co. implemented the idea in some of its plants. Ford estimates only an 8 to 9 percent loss of productive capacity, but a 25 percent reduction in labor.

One U.S. electronics plant (whose management prefers anonymity) proposed its own version of two-shifting, and came up with the same conclusion about capacity; i.e, cutting out the whole third shift was likely to reduce daily output by only 8 percent. The company's study report compares its present three-shift plan with a proposed two-shift plan as follows:

	Three shifts	Two shifts	8:00 A.M.–4:30 P.M. (Maint.: 4:30–8 P.M.) 8:00 P.M.–4:30 A.M. (Maint.: 4:30–8 A.M.)
Gross production hours per day	24.0		16.0
Less (per shift):			
Downtime	1.37		0.40
Allowances:			
Setup/shutdown	0.42		0.16
Unavoidable delays and scheduled breaks	0.67		0.67
Other	1.07		0.87
Work-flow stoppages	0.30		0.15
	3 shifts × $\overline{3.83}$ = 11.5	2 shifts ×	$\overline{2.25}$ = 4.5
Net productive hours per day	12.5		11.5

$$\text{Capacity reduction:} \quad \frac{12.5 - 11.5}{12.5} = \frac{1}{12.5} = 8 \text{ percent}$$

Tangible savings: Lower cost of shift-premium wages
Much less labor—a whole shift; fewer adjustments (some third-shift workers moved to first or second shift)

Intangible savings: Better quality
Machines last longer
More flexibility

Analysis and Innovation

Western line-balancing analysis, item 5 in Figure 6–1, is generally performed by staff engineers and often is elaborate. Mathematical or procedural line-balancing models and computer processing may be employed. The analysis begins with division of the production-line work into small tasks, determination of task time standards, specification of required task sequencing, and notation of physical or other constraints. Then the analysis features a search, among many options, for the line design that minimizes worker delay. If there is a particularly nettlesome bottleneck task in the way of good balance, the methods engineers may work on the task to reduce the time it takes to perform it; then the analysis may be repeated.

Japanese line balancing is not so hemmed in by restrictive assumptions. There is more "see and do" and less formal analysis and off-line modeling. Bottlenecks to good balance are subjected to methods study as a matter of course, not as a special case. Indeed, as has been explained, bottlenecks will be deliberately unearthed by removing workers so that the problems may be eliminated. Thus, Japanese line-balancing study tends to employ thought and ingenuity to change conditions, as opposed to the Western tendency to treat existing conditions mostly as givens.

Line-Balancing Leadership

As has been noted, line-balancing analysis in Western industry is usually a staff engineering function. In Japanese industry foremen will often lead the production line-balancing effort; see item 6 in Figure 6–1. Lacking inventory buffers, the Japanese foremen need to have some line-balancing responsibility so that they can react quickly—by shifting workers around and so forth—when line imbalances crop up as a result of changeover to make a different item or changes in the output rate. Staff analysts and engineers assist when called upon, e.g., for methods-study help or for determining time standards. The Japanese are quite avid about timing and time standards, which foremen need as key input data in rebalancing the line for a changing number of workers, product mix, or output rate.

Quality Problems

Good line balance means full utilization of workers: Keep them busy. The Western imperative to keep workers busy translates into an aversion to stopping or slowing down the line; see item 7 in Figure 6–1. If a station on the line produces a defective unit, that unit is likely to be shunted aside if the defect is serious. Rework lines, touch-up stations, and the like are common adjuncts to Western production lines. Feigenbaum notes that

> The "hidden plant" in U.S. firms may account for from 15 percent to as much as 40 percent of production capacity. By hidden plant I mean personnel and equipment which exists to rework unsatisfactory parts, rework field returns, and reinspect or re-test rejected parts.[5]

In Japanese factories you might have trouble finding rework facilities. While defects are routine events in most Western plants, they are exceptions to be quickly investigated and corrected for in Japanese plants. That means slowing or stopping the line for quality problems, so that those who made the error will have a chance to exercise their responsibility for correcting their own errors (the fifth basic principle of total quality control, introduced in Chapter 3). Workers are not necessarily idled, because some may move to the trouble spot to help diagnose and correct the problem. If the line is slowed ("less-than-full-capacity scheduling" is the facilitating TQC concept, from Chapter 3), some workers may be pulled off and assigned elsewhere for a time; the foreman then quickly rebalances the line with remaining workers by dividing up the tasks differently.

Line Shape

Western production lines tend to be linear or L-shaped; the Japanese like U-shaped or, sometimes, parallel-configured lines; see item 8 in Figure 6–1. Shape preferences are not a matter of aesthetics, but of functionality. Probably the linear and L-shaped lines common in Western plants are that way simply in order to follow the shape of buildings and to provide straight aisles. That rationale is often superseded in Japanese plants by the need for line shapes that make it easy to alter worker assignments.

U-shaped and parallel configurations are particularly suitable, because they allow one worker to handle tasks on both sides of the U or at adjacent stations on parallel line segments, as in an efficiency kitchen. When the scheduled output is high, more workers may be assigned to the line so that a single person would no longer work both sides of the line.

The flexibility afforded by these line shapes is not unknown in the West, as the following discussion of line "topology" shows:

> A ten-machine line might be arranged in a U shape, in which case what might have been the first and last operation might now be as close to one another as the first two or last two. Clearly, the use of such configurations is likely to increase the number of efficient flow patterns available, but this adds to the complexity of the layout problem.[6]

The author is noting the advantages of the U shape almost wistfully, the implication being that one might not want to try it because of the added analytical complexity.

The preference for U-shaped lines and parallel line segments is particularly strong in the Toyota family of companies.[7] The Toyota people also have a current preference for line-segment lengths of about five work stations in production lines fabricating or subassembling components. That is, the normal number of workers on the line segment would be five. But when the line

141

changes over to make a simpler part or the output rate drops, four, three, or two workers, or even one, can run the line—and without much walk time, since U-shapes and parallel line segments provide clustering of work stations. But, of course, the number of operations per worker required to make the type of part the line is designed for may naturally suggest more or fewer stations than five. If the natural number of stations for reasonable balance is, say, two or three, Toyota's preference is to find another two-station or three-station line segment to locate parallel to the first. The parallel lines offer more staffing options.

Movement of Materials

Another aspect of line topography is distance between stations, item 9 in Figure 6–1. The Japanese prefer to position manned stations close enough together that pieces may be handed from one worker to the next without walking. As was noted in an earlier chapter, the Japanese view is that conveyors are an undesirable expense (and also frowned upon because they hold inventory and are subject to breakdown), which can be avoided by close station positioning.

The Western attitude seems to be that conveyors are desirable. They have the semblance of efficiency.

Equipment

The Japanese gain flexibility by a preference for multiple copies of a small, inexpensive, special-purpose, self-developed machine, rather than large multipurpose commercial machines; see item 10 in Figure 6–1. It may seem contradictory to suggest that special-purpose machines can be more flexible than multipurpose machines. Not so. If a need exists for making, say, 1,000 parts per day, a Japanese company might have its toolmakers develop five small special-purpose machines, each with a capacity of around 200 parts per day; the Western company would probably buy one large high-priced multipurpose machine with a capacity in excess of 1,000 parts per day. Smaller, self-made machines can run smaller lots of different parts, can be easily maintained one at a time, can be staffed variously, and can be added to (or dismantled or modified) one by one. By contrast, "super-machines" tend to take on inordinate importance, so that whole lines, work schedules, and sales efforts are geared to their needs and limitations.

Scope of Production-Line Applications

The very idea of a production line is, in Western industry, associated mostly with high-volume, labor-intensive final assembly, not fabrication; see item 11 in Figure 6–1. (However, there are a few industries in which a small number of component parts are made into a large variety of end products. In such cases even Western plants are likely to employ production lines in the component parts fabrication stage of manufacture.) Laborers are inherently flexible and, on some Western final assembly lines, are able to adjust rather easily to a sequence of changing models.

By contrast, the Japanese design flexibility into even the capital-intensive processes, such as subassembly and parts fabrication, which may then be configured as production lines. The many advantages are presented in the Chapter 2 discussion of JIT/TQC production.

Mixed Models

The final item in Figure 6–1 is the running of mixed models through a production line, a complex topic requiring more extensive discussion. Mixed-model production seems to be far more

143

common in Japanese plants than in Western plants making the same products. Mixed-model production in Japan is found mostly in final assembly, where it is easiest to achieve. Japanese industry is steadily pushing mixed-model production into subassembly and fabrication as well. By contrast, in the West mixed-model production is virtually unheard of, and in many industries it is unthinkable outside of final assembly.

The characteristics and advantages of mixed-model production depend on whether it is in operation only in final assembly, or in final assembly plus some of the processes feeding parts to final assembly. First, let us consider the case of final assembly only.

Mixed Models in Final Assembly

Prenting and Thomopoulos write that "the advantages of mixed model assembly are numerous: it provides a continuous flow of each model, reduces finished goods inventory, eliminates line changeover, and provides greater flexibility in production."[8] Continuous flow of models and reduced inventory of finished goods are clear and important advantages, but the other two points seem more to be *conditions* for use of mixed-model production than advantages. For example, key reasons why the Japanese are able to widely employ the mixed-model concept are (1) their attacks upon changeover, or setup, time and (2) their production flexibility: flexible labor; foreman-level control of balancing/rebalancing, labor assignment, and line speedup/slowdown; U-shaped and parallel lines, with stations close together; and multiple copies of small machines.

In Western industry mixed-model production is most likely to be found in final assembly of autos, trucks, tractors, and sometimes consumer appliances. A family of similar models may be run down a single assembly line in any order. The materials control staff pre-plans the arrival of major component parts and

144

places ample stocks of smaller parts close to the line (e.g., the "Kelvinator system" of running mixed models of refrigerators). Assemblers may experience delays in searching to locate the right part for the model at hand. Thus, in general, mixed-model assembly is thought to be characterized by lower productivity—more labor and inventory per unit—than single-model assembly.

The Japanese approach to mixed-model assembly lines is more disciplined. Color coding (one color for all parts-containers and labels for a given model) is often used to cut down search time; precise positioning of feeder parts-racks has the same purpose. Kanban may be employed to match parts usage with parts delivery and parts production, to cut down on inventory in support of the assembly line.

Mixed Models in Subassembly and Fabrication

In running mixed models where there is more equipment and less labor, e.g., in subassembly and fabrication processes, the Japanese rely less on discipline and more on task timing, sequencing, and balance. Task timing becomes critical if machines are doing part of the work, because machine times are quite fixed and precise and therefore a dominant factor.

For example, the task of boring holes in a large pump housing may take twice as long to set up and run as doing the same thing with a small pump housing. Western manufacturers see, in such a situation, intolerable imbalance, and therefore they generally put the mixed-model idea quickly out of mind and resort to batches of first one size and then the other (sometimes called multimodel production). The Japanese approach is first to attack the setup time, which melts away part of the imbalance between models. Then imbalance in run times (in this case, for hole boring) can be treated by sequencing.[9]

A hypothetical example, again for boring holes in large (L) and small (S) pump housings, follows:

145

GIVEN:

Scheduled output per day: 24 large + 24 small = 48 per day
Run times: 12 minutes per large unit, 8 minutes per small unit
Assume negligible setup time

BALANCED MIXED-MODEL SEQUENCE:

Model sequence	L L	S S S	L L	L L	S S S	
Operation time	12 12	8 8 8	12 12	12 12	8 8 8	Repeats
	24	24	24	24	24	4 times
			120			per day

As the example shows, the mixed-model schedule is perfectly balanced. There are five 24-minute mini-cycles for each of the four 120-minute main cycles per day, and the schedule yields the desired 24 large and 24 small housings per day.

The grand ideal is to run mixed models in final assembly, which has been fed by mixed-model or dedicated subassembly and fabrication lines running about the same mix of models. Inventories are thus cut to the bone, with all the attendant JIT/TQC benefits. Few Japanese manufacturers have gone very far in achieving the grand ideal, but they are working on it. Western industry virtually does not view the objective as within the realm of possibility.

Mixed Models Compared with Overlapped Production

If a plant is configured to run mixed models, idle in-process inventory may be reduced to a negligible amount. My students have wondered if it is possible to obtain the same in-process-inventory reductions through overlapped production of lots. The answer is yes, but at the expense of under-utilizing capacity in subassembly and fabrication. Figures 6–2 and 6–3 serve to illustrate, using pump manufacturing as an example.

Figure 6–2. Mixed-Model Production

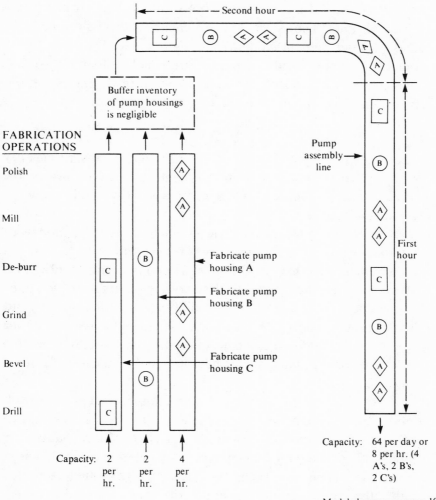

147

Figure 6–2 depicts a mixed-model pump assembly line, plus fabrication lines to machine the cast housings that the pump goes into. (Not shown are other subassembly and fabrication lines that would provide pumps, gaskets, bolts, and so forth to the pump assembly line.) The assembly line's capacity is 64 pumps per day; that is, 8 per hour: 4 model-A pumps, 2 model-B pumps, and 2 model-C pumps. Model-A pumps are small and simple so that two can be made in the same time as one B or C. Therefore, the mixed-model assembly sequence is:

A A B C A A B C . . .

There is a model changeover every 10 minutes, or six times per hour, and model changeover time is negligible. Two hours' worth of production in process on the pump assembly line is shown in Figure 6–2.

There is one fabrication line for each of the three models of pump housing. Fabrication consists of: (1) drill holes for bolts in the steel castings that are to house the pump, (2) bevel, (3) grind, (4) de-burr, (5) mill, (6) polish. Each of the three fabrication lines is equipped and staffed to run steadily all day long, turning out housings at the same rate as they are used in pump assembly: four A's, two B's, and two C's per hour. There is virtually no buffer inventory of housings, since they are used at the same rate as they are made.

Now let us consider the same example, except with each model run as a lot in final assembly; see Figure 6–3. This is known as a multimodel instead of a mixed-model line. Model changeover time is still assumed to be negligible. That is, the assembly line is exactly the same as in Figure 6–2; it is merely sequenced in lots rather than mixed models. Productivity in final assembly is also exactly the same: an output rate of 64 pumps per day with the same inputs.

Productivity in the three fabrication centers, however, is much worse, because each of the fabrication lines now must be designed to provide pump housings at peak rates that are triple

Figure 6–3. Overlapped Production

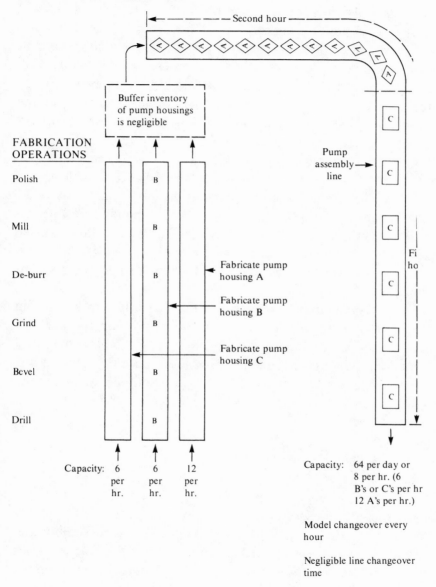

Second hour

Buffer inventory
of pump housings
is negligible

FABRICATION
OPERATIONS

Polish

Mill

De-burr

Grind

Bevel

Drill

Fabricate pump
housing A

Fabricate pump
housing B

Fabricate pump
housing C

Pump
assembly→
line

Capacity: 6   6   12
          per   per   per
          hr.   hr.   hr.

Capacity: 64 per day or
            8 per hr. (6
            B's or C's per hr
            12 A's per hr.)

Model changeover every
hour

Negligible line changeover
time

149

those of Figure 6–2. Specifically, the capacities in Figure 6–3 are twelve A's, six B's, and six C's per hour, versus four A's, two B's, and two C's per hour in Figure 6–2. Since the pump assembly line schedule calls for only one model to be run per hour, then only one model of pump housing is needed per hour; the other two pump housing lines shut down while the given model is run. For example, for the point in time represented by Figure 6–3, fabrication of B is in progress since B-pump assembly is about to begin; but the A and C fabrication lines are idle. As a whole, the fabrication lines run at only one-third of their capacity in support of lot-oriented assembly (Figure 6–3), but at full capacity in support of mixed models (Figure 6–2).

Figure 6–3 by no means shows the full extent of losses in productivity resulting from assembly in lots. Numerous other components go into the assembled pump—the pump itself, fasteners, gaskets, controls, labels, covers, and so on. Many of these components would be designed to fit only one of the pump models, which means off-and-on rather than steady component fabrication.

A feasible alternative is to run the fabrication lines just as in Figure 6–2, but with buffer inventories built up for the two models not being assembled at a given time. But buffer-inventory idleness produces the same undesirable effects as fabrication-line idleness: less productivity, i.e., more resource inputs for the same outputs.[10]

Mixed Models and Suppliers

An outside company supplying parts to a manufacturer assembling mixed models is in a position to gain productivity advantages for itself, just as the assembler's own subassembly and fabrication centers do. Furthermore, the outside supplier's fortunes may become more closely linked to those of the assembly plant—a healthy mutual-dependency relationship.

Suppose, for example, that a supplier has a contract with Kawasaki to supply a turn signal used only on the largest motorcycle model, the KZ1300. If Kawasaki assembles, say, one KZ1300 every 30 minutes on a mixed-model line, the turn-signal supplier can keep producing the signals at exactly the same steady rate and deliver them often so that virtually no inventory is built up. If, on the other hand, Kawasaki runs a batch of KZ1300s once a week, the supplier would need to build inventory in one-week batches. In such situations the supplier's tendency is to develop a super turn-signal fabrication center capable of producing the whole week's supply in perhaps one day or less. The supplier then seeks business from other companies to keep the turn-signal work center busy the other four days of the work week. The supplier becomes a job shop producing in job lots; JIT benefits—quality, low scrap, and so on—are out the window, and the allegiance of the turn-signal supplier is divided among several customers rather than being dedicated to just one.

Applications

The Chapter 5 discussion of plant configurations noted some of the steps Kawasaki, Lincoln, has taken toward Japanese-style production line operations. Some of those points are reiterated and elaborated upon here in reference to the problems of line design and balance.

Flexibility and the Labor Union

In spring and summer of 1981 the Kawasaki plant was receiving a steady stream of visitors from other U.S. plants. Most of the visitors were more or less struck by the flexibility of the Kawasaki work force, who are moved around from job to job as the work

151

load fluctuates and as bottlenecks occur. Most visitors were from unionized plants, and the visit to Kawasaki simply reinforced their dichotomous stereotype of unionized workers as being inflexible whereas nonunion workers are flexible. The stereotype blurs judgment. There are many nonunion plants in the United States, and in these plants workers are indeed likely to be moved around from job to job considerably more than in union plants. But the purposes and benefits of worker mobility in these plants are far different from those in Japanese-owned plants like Kawasaki:

1. In the typical nonunion U.S. plant, workers are moved to keep them busy, to keep equipment busy, to replenish parts in low supply, to handle a crisis, or to fill a hot order—all of which are unplanned "fire-fighting" purposes.

2. At Kawasaki, Lincoln (and in Japan), workers are moved in support of a grand JIT/TQC production-line strategy, which includes tactics such as:

a. Move workers out to avoid making parts before they are needed (better to let workers twiddle their thumbs).

b. Move workers out to avoid making items that might be defective (slow down the line—run it with fewer workers—until problems are corrected).

c. Reduce the number of workers assigned to a smoothly running production line in order to expose and deal with the problems exposed by the reduction.

d. Move assemblers into production of component parts needed in support of final assembly, and component producers into final assembly when the assembly schedule calls for it.

e. Move workers into facilities construction, equipment modification, and maintenance tasks, as needed.

An evening news story carried by the major TV networks in the United States testifies to Kawasaki's commitment not to build inventories. The reports noted that Kawasaki had lent 11 of its excess workers to the City of Lincoln, at full pay, for an indeterminate time period beginning in October 1981. The reasons for such unprecedented generosity were a low recessionary demand, coupled with a preference for no inventory buildup and no layoffs.

In contrast is another nonunion manufacturing company several miles down the road from the Kawasaki plant. The company, a producer of wooden power pole crossbars, also had the benevolent policy of avoiding layoffs. The company's response to a large drop in demand in 1980–1981 was to keep everyone on the payroll making crossbars for inventory. By late 1981 the company had nearly two years' supply of crossbars!

Kawasaki wants to keep the union out, and so far the United Auto Workers have lost at the ballot box in two elections concerning approval of the union as official bargaining agent. But all is not lost when employees go union. Perhaps half of the major Japanese plants in the United States have done so: e.g., Sanyo in Arkansas, Sharp in Tennessee, and part of the Honda work force in Ohio. Union workers are like anyone else. They want their companies to be highly productive, profitable, and stable. But if the production-management system is so ineffectual as to allow or even encourage carelessness and waste—e.g., making parts that aren't needed, failing to keep equipment in nearly perfect condition, keeping the line running even when quality problems are surfacing—the attitudes of the workers and their union, if any, turn negative. At Kawasaki it is obvious to the workers that their mobility within the plant directly contributes to productivity; my guess is that nothing else is as important to securing labor's cooperation.

Line Design and Operation

Kawasaki has adopted several other of the Japanese production line management tendencies shown in Figure 6–1. In an earlier

153

chapter it was noted that foremen have played leadership roles in projects to reconfigure and rebuild the dedicated frame welding lines and the KLT differential subassembly line. Kawasaki, Lincoln, has a large number of punch presses, all of the same brand (Bliss), which is a Japanese way of gaining flexibility and reducing problems of maintenance and supply of parts for the equipment. And Kawasaki has adopted the Japanese attitude that conveyors are to be avoided: Large conveyor systems to move tires and gas tanks were taken out of service in fall 1981.

It is probably in final street bike assembly that Kawasaki most visibly departs from typical Western practices. Earlier remarks about the line may be reiterated: The line is strung with help and stop lights; workers are moved out to cause more lights to go on, exposing trouble spots; feeder parts racks are placed with precision, color-coded, and stocked by means of kanban; and the line is running fully mixed models. Mixed-model scheduling, which had been little more than a dream in summer 1981, was fully implemented by January 1982. The lights and the positioning and color-coding of racks were important preparatory steps. Whereas a given model had been run in multimodel quantities of 200, the line now may change models unit by unit.

Conclusions

A production line is a complex assemblage of workers, managers, and advisers; parts, tools, and machines; handling devices; spatial constraints; attitudes and goals; and a host of potential problems. Given such complexity, production-line design and operation is more art than science. Tendencies of Western manufacturers to manage production lines one way and Japanese manufacturers to manage them another way have been noted. The Japanese system encourages flexibility; the Western system encourages workers to "protect their turf."

The list of Western vs. Japanese tendencies (Figure 6–1) is intentionally dichotomous. Few companies will see their own practices as falling nicely into either list; there is a gray area between. As a prescription for Western industry, the list of Japanese production-line tendencies is not suitable for all cases. For example, mixed-model production is not needed when the production rate for a given part is very high—say, thousands per day. Many of the specific points made in this chapter should be considered as suggestive, and the nature of the company should guide its own custom-tailored approach. But the general notion of a system designed for flexibility has universal appeal.

In conclusion, the following may serve as a restatement of the sixth lesson:

Western workers are overspecialized; Japanese-style labor flexibility is the key to effective resource management.

CHAPTER 7

Just-in-Time Purchasing

LESSON 7: Travel light and make numerous trips—like the water beetle.

The Japanese by no means confine the JIT concept to in-plant production. Purchased inventories are considered as evil as in-plant inventories. Therefore, the JIT concept as applied to purchasing translates into frequent releases or authorizations and frequent deliveries. My Japanese acquaintances liken their parts delivery practices to the water beetle, which is light enough to float on top of the water and make numerous swift trips across the pond.

Also, the Japanese tend to buy from the same few suppliers year after year, so that the suppliers develop a competency that is particularly attuned to the delivery and quality needs of the buying firm. Confidence in the supplier reduces buffer inventories carried in the buying plant to quantities that sometimes are used up in only a few hours, with a delivery frequency from the supplier of more than once a day. And over time, some suppliers achieve quality levels high enough for all receiving inspections to be bypassed; in Japan, the supplier may even be directed to deliver right to the production line rather than to a receiving dock.

A typical reaction to these stories by people who are steeped in U.S. purchasing practices is, if not disbelief, complete confidence that it "won't work here." In this chapter I explain how certain aspects of JIT purchasing *can* work and are in fact in operation in the U.S. purchasing environment. The ideal of zero inventory by means of one-at-a-time continuous delivery from supplier to user is a pipedream—in Japan as well as here. But relentless attack upon delivery lot sizes and relentless search for ways to overcome the freight economics of full truckload and carload lots is a Japanese approach that we can and should emulate.

The discussion of JIT purchasing focuses primarily on the Kawasaki, Lincoln, plant. Kawasaki appears to be the first U.S. plant to formally establish a JIT purchasing program. We shall also look at some less formalized examples of JIT buying at other Japanese subsidiaries in this country, and at the budding JIT purchasing efforts in the U.S. auto industry.

Initiation

Kawasaki initiated JIT production and inventory control on the factory floor in early 1980. Later in that year JIT buying was formally launched in the purchasing department. However, one of Kawasaki's suppliers, TRI-CON, had been supplying motorcycle seats on a just-in-time basis—typically two deliveries a day —since the TRI-CON plant begain operations in Lincoln in 1977. TRI-CON, a subsidiary of Tokyo Seating Co., simply followed the pattern typical of supplier firms in Japan: Move close to the "parent" plant and deliver high-quality goods frequently and in small quantities.

The plant manager, Mr. Butt, and a Japanese adviser who

was experienced in Japanese purchasing, Mr. Akasada, provided impetus to get the JIT purchasing program started in 1980. Mr. Claunch, a young purchasing manager, took the initiative with enthusiasm—after having become indoctrinated in Japanese buying practices himself. One of Claunch's first steps was to formally train his purchasing staff in JIT concepts. Imbued with the JIT purchasing mode of operating, Kawasaki buyers today are gradually expanding the application of JIT buying to a larger number of suppliers.

A number of characteristics and benefits of JIT purchasing to be discussed are summarized, in list form, in Table 7–1.

TABLE 7–1.   JIT Purchasing: Characteristics and Benefits

JIT Characteristics

Quantities:

> Steady output rate (a desirable prerequisite)
> Frequent deliveries in small quantities
> Long-term contracts, e.g., blanket orders
> Minimal release paper
> Delivery quantities variable from delivery to delivery but fixed for whole contract term
> Little or no overage or underage acceptable
> Suppliers encouraged to package in exact quantities
> Suppliers encouraged to reduce their production-lot sizes

Quality:

> Minimal specs
> Suppliers helped to meet quality requirements
> Close relationships between buyers' and suppliers' QC people
> Suppliers encouraged to use process control instead of inspection

Suppliers:

> Few suppliers
> Nearby suppliers

TABLE 7–1. (*cont.*)

___

Active use of value analysis to enable desirable suppliers to become/stay price-competitive

Clusters of remote suppliers

Repeat business with same suppliers

Competitive bidding mostly limited to new part numbers

Buyer plant's resistance to vertical integration and subsequent wipeout of supplier business

Suppliers encouraged to extend JIT buying to *their* suppliers

Shipping:

Scheduling inbound freight

Gaining control by use of company-owned or contract shipping, contract warehousing, and trailers for freight consolidation/storage where possible—instead of common carriers

JIT Benefits

Costs of parts:

Low inventory-carrying cost

Decreasing cost of parts, because of long-term learning curve benefits in use of limited suppliers

Low scrap cost, since defects are detected early

Quality:

Fast detection of defects, since deliveries are frequent

Fast correction of defects, since supplier setups are frequent and lots are small

Less need for inspection (of lots), since process control is encouraged

Higher quality of parts purchased—and of products they go into

Design:

Fast response to engineering changes

Design innovativeness, since suppliers are expert and not hamstrung by restrictive specs

160

Administrative efficiency:

Few requests for bids
Few suppliers to contract with
Contracts negotiated infrequently
Minimal release paperwork
Little expediting
Short travel and telephone distances and costs
Simple accounting for parts received, if suppliers use standard containers
Reliable identification of incoming orders, if suppliers use thorough container labeling

Productivity:

Reduced rework
Reduced inspection
Reduced delay because of off-spec parts, late deliveries, or delivery underages
Reduced purchasing, production control, inventory control, and supervision, with more reliable parts provisioning and smaller quantities carried

---

The JIT characteristics are in four groups: (1) *quantities:* product outputs, parts inputs, contracts administered, and purchasing paperwork; (2) *quality:* specifications, coordination, and control; (3) *suppliers:* number, location, size, longevity, and assistance/ advice offered; (4) *shipping:* inbound freight and freight/storage modes. All of the JIT features in Table 7–1 have been put into effect by Kawasaki, Lincoln, to one extent or another, and therefore seem feasible for at least some U.S. manufacturers. The JIT benefits are in five groups: (1) *costs of parts:* carrying, learning-curve decreases, and scrap; (2) *quality:* detection, correction, process control, and overall quality; (3) *design:* response time and innovativeness; (4) *administrative efficiency:* few suppliers, bids and contracts, minimal expediting and release paper, and simple communications and receiving; (5) *productivity:* less rework, inspection, and parts-related delay, and more staff support.

The JIT characteristics listed in Table 7–1 are interrelated, and JIT benefits listed in the table tend to grow as more JIT buying features are implemented. The interrelationships and pattern of growth of benefits are discussed in the following sections, not point by point but in logical clusters.

Training Buyers

The JIT training that Mr. Claunch gave consisted of five one-hour classes. All of the purchasing department—four buyers, one traffic manager, one traffic coordinator, and the clerical staff—went through this training. Also, Claunch's supervisor, Mr. Polivka, the materials manager, sat in on the set of training sessions.

Training materials were pieced together: some from an Arthur Andersen and Co. seminar that Claunch attended (Arthur Andersen had been conducting seminars around the country on Japanese manufacturing methods); some based on internal contacts with Mr. Butt and Mr. Akasada; and some based on collected publications.

Early in the course one buyer said something like "I see—what we are trying to do is work off somebody else's inventory." But later in the course it became clear to the class that under JIT, suppliers also benefit, especially from long-term contracts and stable relationships with the buying plant, which are an important element of JIT buying. By making parts steadily rather than in batches, the supplier realizes inventory, quality, and scrap improvements: Defects are caught early, and there are fewer defectives to throw out or rework. Further inventory benefits may be gained if the supplier also initiates JIT buying from its own suppliers. TRI-CON, the seat supplier, for example, is committed to JIT buying of the materials from which it makes motorcycle seats. A less obvious but potentially great benefit to the supplier is less need for large, expensive equipment—and steadier utilization of existing equipment—since the supplier may produce in the same steady daily amounts as are called for in the JIT purchase agreement. (See the related discussion in Chapter 6 under the heading "Mixed Models Compared with Overlapped Production.")

The benefits of JIT buying are greatest in the case of materials used every day. For materials whose usage rates are irregular, you can go only so far toward frequent deliveries in small amounts, but the point is to try to go that far.

Missionary Work

The job of a buyer in industrial purchasing is to find good suppliers, arrange purchase agreements, and then follow up to assure compliance. This normally involves a small amount of "missionary" work: for example, shaping up the supplier to adjust to the buying plant's quality, delivery, and service requirements. For Kawasaki buyers, the missionary work has become extensive, because they are trying to provide their suppliers with JIT education, leading to JIT purchase orders.

In spring 1981 Kawasaki buyers spread the JIT message to plant representatives of some 40 suppliers. One approach has been to schedule a "vendor day." Marketing representatives from supplier plants meet at Kawasaki for presentations on the rationale behind JIT. By summer 1981, more serious JIT discussions had reached the top management levels of about eight supplier plants. At least three or four discussions were generally required before a JIT agreement could be worked out.

In one case the supplier plant initiated the JIT discussions. Mr. Strouf, president of Dico Co. in Des Moines, contacted Kawasaki, saying that he had heard or read about its approach and wished to discuss it. Mr. Strouf visited Mr. Claunch in Lincoln, and with little further ado a JIT agreement was established. Dico supplies wheel rims and tires mounted for Kawasaki's three-wheel (KLT) recreational bike; in view of the distance, freight costs dictate that deliveries be in whole truckloads, which translates into a delivery frequency of every three days. A three-day delivery interval is not just-in-time, but compared with the prior delivery interval, measured in weeks—typical U.S. large-lot buying—the interval approaches JIT.

JIT Purchasing Agreements

In Japan it is common for a JIT purchase agreement to involve a rather small amount of paper. For example, the purchase order (PO) or contract may specify (in addition to price and engineering data) an overall quantity simply to be delivered during a period of several months in accordance with a long-term production schedule provided by the buying plant.

Some Japanese OEM (original-equipment manufacturing) companies use kanban (order cards) instead of a production schedule to trigger deliveries. The kanban are released from the using work center on the shop floor of the OEM company: deliveries are thus matched with the work center's rate of usage and hence are closer to being just-in-time than would be the case if they were based on a production schedule. The kanban may serve as the invoice when returned with the parts to the OEM plant. The quantity of cards are totaled, and the total is payable perhaps once a month.

At Kawasaki, Lincoln, there is a bit more purchase paper than that, e.g., invoices and packing lists. One reason is to provide a good audit trail for accounting purposes. But "release paper" is minimal. Typically, a blanket PO is issued for a production season. The PO specifies specific delivery dates. Whenever delivery dates change, a change notice is issued to the supplier. Some daily variation in the delivery quantity is provided for. For example, every morning a Kawasaki buyer phones TRI-CON to

164

state the quantity of seats to be delivered that day. If Kawasaki has produced fewer motorcycles the previous day than scheduled, there will be seats left over; therefore, today's morning call will request fewer seats for today's production.

JIT Specifications

Another notable feature of the Japanese system of industrial buying is simplicity of the product specifications (specs) that suppliers bid to or make to. In preparing design data for parts to be purchased, U.S. engineers tend to specify and develop tolerances for just about every conceivable design feature of the end product. Purchasing merely passes the specs on to the bidders, and expects bidders to comply exactly. The Japanese way, which is followed by Kawasaki, Lincoln, is to rely more on performance specifications and less on design specifications. Kawasaki buyers sometimes ask suppliers for recommendations, rather than rigidly specifying. The idea is to let a supplier innovate and also to allow the buyer some discretion in evaluating the supplier's proposals. After all, the supplier is the expert. You have elected to buy rather than make it yourself, so why not rely on the supplier's expertise?

A performance-oriented spec package might consist of a blueprint with only critical dimensions. Type of material may need to be specified, but sometimes strength characteristics, type of finish, and so forth are sufficient. Even the finish may not need to be precisely specified: Kawasaki calls for only "an appropriate polymer coating" on some parts. The spec package avoids restrictions that dictate how the product is to be made, leaving the supplier some freedom of choice on whether to stamp or drill, cast or weld, grind or mill.

Both Kawasaki and TRI-CON have found a good deal of surprise and some resistance to the minimal-specs idea among

U.S. suppliers. For example, TRI-CON buys seat pans based on blueprints that call for 12-gauge cold rolled steel, give key dimensions, and describe the desired finish—but give no other specifications. One Detroit firm that wanted to bid on some work for TRI-CON was flabbergasted at the lack of specs and backed off.

Minimal specs contribute toward JIT buying in that specification-related delays and work stoppages may be dealt with quickly and without great formality in the supplier's plant. (And minimal specs in the user's own plant improve JIT production as well, because foremen, engineers, and quality control people can resolve some design problems as they occur on the factory floor.) It becomes easier for the supplier to keep making and delivering steadily in small amounts.

Exact Quantities

It is common practice for U.S. suppliers to ship somewhat more or less than the quantity called for in the purchase agreement. On the buyer's receiving dock, the goods must be counted to see how many to pay for. The buyer plant may refuse the shipment if the quantity is too far off—which typically means an overage or underage of more than 10 percent.

The Japanese JIT concept permits no such variability. The Japanese buyer expects—and gets—an exact quantity or very close to it. The Japanese commonly use packages or containers with a standard number of divided spaces or an exact cube, which makes it easy to count out the right number. Japanese parts packaging is also much better labeled and more protective than is usual in the United States. There is therefore less need for extra parts as a cushion for damage, and less chance for misidentification—both of which are important considerations in JIT buying.

Kawasaki, Lincoln, receives truckloads of parts from Japan every day. Most are boxed in knocked-down (KD) kits of 200,

166

and the quantity is so certain that the parts from Japan are not counted. By contrast, nearly all parts from U.S. suppliers must still be counted. Kawasaki's buyers hope to convince the U.S. suppliers to use Japanese-style packing and to make it clear that quantities must be exact.

Purchase-Lot Sizes

In deciding how much of a given material to buy at a time, the buyer could go to the textbooks and find an economic purchase quantity (EPQ) formula (which is similar to the economic order quantity formula, referred to in an earlier chapter, for determining lot sizes for goods made in-house). The textbooks tell us to use the average cost of processing a purchase order as one input into the economic purchase quantity equation. Actually, the advice is dubious for two reasons: (1) Most purchasing departments are often able to undercut the average order-processing cost through use of a variety of techniques: blanket orders, systems contracting, stockless purchasing, approved supplier lists, petty cash, and so forth. (2) Quite often the cost of freight handling acts as the most limiting factor in lot sizing. That is, it often does not pay to ship in less-than-truckload or less-than-carload amounts, and therefore material may be shipped less often in larger amounts than is otherwise desirable.

Factor 1 leads to lower purchase quantities and factor 2 leads to higher quantities than the EPQ would yield. I suppose that on the average, the two factors tend to cancel each other out, so that on the average the EPQ seems nearly correct. But each given item to be bought has its own characteristics, which may favor factor 1 but not factor 2, or vice versa. Therefore, the astute buyer pays little attention to EPQ formulas and focuses instead on the nature of the product to be bought, and on opportunities to save administrative or shipping costs.

167

The point I am leading up to is that JIT buying—obtaining small quantities frequently—is consistent with the U.S. purchasing practices of blanket orders, systems contracting, and so on aimed at cutting administrative red tape. But where JIT buying and U.S. practices part company is over the issue of shipping costs. American buyers take shipping costs and the whole freight-handling system to be a given, which tends to force large-lot buying. JIT buying, like JIT production, considers any such obstacles to cutting lot sizes as a challenge rather than a given. The freight system may be attacked in various ways, and distances to suppliers must become an important consideration in selecting them. These issues are examined further in the next sections.

Inbound Freight

The typical U.S. way of dealing with inbound freight is to leave it up to the supplier and the transportation industry. This is true even for materials bought "FOB shipping point," in which the buying plant owns and absorbs carrying charges on the goods from the date of shipment. The JIT purchasing philosophy aims at assuring steady, reliable incoming deliveries; the idea is to avoid excess carrying charges for goods that arrive early or are stuck somewhere in the shipping system (on a railroad siding, at a break-bulk storage point, in a half-full truck), and perhaps, more importantly, to avoid disruptions in the buyer's plant when goods arrive late.

JIT buying can hardly be successful if inbound freight scheduling is left up to the transportation system, whose primary concern is with optimal utilization of drivers, storage space, and trailer or rail-car cubes. Therefore, scheduling of inbound freight has become a purchasing department function in the Kawasaki approach to JIT buying. The traffic manager works under the purchasing manager, whose duties include inbound freight—as opposed to the usual U.S. practice, in which traffic handles only outbound freight.

In some cases, Kawasaki's supplier is responsible for deliveries. In such cases there is little inbound freight scheduling to be done, because the JIT purchase agreements will specify not shipping dates or times but delivery dates or times; supplier responsibility for meeting the delivery schedules lets the buyer sidestep battles with commercial common carriers. Another way of reducing inbound freight scheduling problems is to try to deal with clusters of vendors rather than widely scattered ones, so that freight may be consolidated daily (or more often) in economical full trailer loads or carloads. Vendor clusters also afford increased use of contract shipping or company-owned trucks and use of trailers as portable warehouses. These measures improve control over freight scheduling and make it possible to avoid the uncertainties of dealing with break-bulk warehouses.

Secondary Benefits of JIT Purchasing

The most apparent benefit of JIT buying is, as the Kawasaki buyer put it, "working off somebody else's inventory." In monetary terms, this means reducing your own carrying costs: cost of capital tied up in inventory plus storage cost. Equally important are the scrap/quality and productivity benefits, discussed earlier. When all the "bells and whistles" are in place, there can be several other benefits, which tend to act together—a symbiotic relationship.

One such benefit, which was briefly mentioned, is reduced paperwork. Conventional lot-size economics has it that smaller lots mean more orders per year to process and therefore *more* paperwork and order-processing cost. But the environment in which JIT buying best functions is one in which (1) the buyer's production schedules are relatively level so that demand for bought materials is steady and predictable; (2) supplier excellence and loyalty is encouraged by giving larger, steadier orders to a smaller number of suppliers; and (3) long-term purchase agreements provide for frequent deliveries with minimal paperwork. With smooth demand, few suppliers, and long-term agreements, paperwork costs may be lower rather than higher.

For a supplier, happiness is having a contract that is exclusive (or nearly so), long-term, and invariable, which, as has been suggested, are the characteristics of a JIT purchase agreement. Such a contract affords the supplier the opportunity to shave peak capacity, retain a trained labor force, and cut its own inventories, possibly through JIT buying from its own suppliers.

Proximity of Suppliers to Buyers

Related to all this are the mutual benefits that are realized when the supplier locates close to the buyer's plant. For both buyer and supplier, the closer the JIT agreement comes to piece-for-piece delivery, the greater the savings in inventory carrying cost and other benefits. But pure piece-for-piece delivery is rarely justifiable, because such small quantities are likely to violate the economics of unit-load transportation.

At the extreme, a unit load may be a supertanker of crude oil, a barge-load of wheat, or a unit train of coal. Such extremely large economic loads apply where the distance is great (and the quantity large). The economics of a unit load melt away as the distance is decreased. For example, if you build a power-generating plant in a coalfield, you can use conveyors to *continuously* feed the coal to heat the boilers—rather than delivering coal load by load. The point is that unit-load economics may be overcome by cutting the transportation distance between supplier and buyer plants.

Kawasaki, Lincoln's seat supplier, TRI-CON, chose to locate only two miles away. (In 1982, TRI-CON started up a second

U.S. plant near to its other major American customer, Honda, in Marysville, Ohio.) Kawasaki is aggressively seeking to establish long-term relationships with a few other potential suppliers in the Lincoln area. The local suppliers often initially lack the capability to make the parts Kawasaki wants with the requisite quality. Kawasaki's buyers, along with the engineers and quality control people, have taken it upon themselves to work with potential suppliers to overcome the deficiencies. In time, a potential supplier receives a few small orders; if satisfactory, large blanket contracts follow.

Coordination Benefits

When a supplier plant is geographically near the buyer plant, there are numerous coordination benefits besides the shipment cost advantages. Long-distance telephone charges may be avoided, which encourages more communication between all parties. When the supplier is in the same telephone zone, it is not uncommon, for example, for the JIT buyer to phone the supplier every day in order to effect slight adjustments in the daily delivery quantity, as Kawasaki does for seat deliveries from TRI-CON.

Perhaps even more significant are the benefits of closer coordination on engineering and quality matters. When the supplier plant is nearby, engineers and QC people may frequently visit each other's plants. Engineering questions may be quickly resolved, and potential quality problems may be nipped in the bud. As has been mentioned, the overall concept of just-in-time seems to hinge nearly as much on preventing production of defective large lots as on cutting inventories. This is the case for JIT as applied to parts bought from suppliers, as well as parts made in-house. In the case of parts bought from suppliers, frequent deliveries will assure that defects are discovered early; but if the plants are far apart, the economic advantages of full trailer-load or carload shipping enter in, which precludes the possibility of the

171

buyer discovering bad parts before many are made and shipped. Also, lack of close engineering/QC coordination is likely to mean a relatively frequent occurrence of such defect conditions and low effectiveness in resolving the problems.

Related to all this is the use of minimal specs. With freedom from restrictive specs, supplier and buyer engineering staffs can be in frequent contact regarding which product features are really essential; and innovative, low-cost ways to get around troublesome production and quality difficulties can be developed with little delay or paperwork.

Thus, a virtue of geographical proximity is that the supplier tends to acquire status—in the eyes of the buyer—for its high quality and design responsiveness. The risk of a supplier's having its contract canceled after the expense of building next to the buyer is lessened because the buyer depends increasingly on the supplier's quality as well as responsiveness.

Value Analysis Benefits

Value analysis, a respected U.S. purchasing practice that sometimes falls into neglect, may have new life breathed into it in connection with JIT buying. In negotiating a JIT purchase agreement, the potential supplier receives the buyer's blueprints with minimal specs and comes back with a bid price. If the price is too high (or even if it isn't), the buyer may visit the supplier's plant to go over the bid in detail—an informal value analysis. The object is to see just where the highest costs are for the supplier; often the buyer can bend even the minimal specs in such a way as to save the supplier some money, thus reducing the bid. ("Loose" specifications similarly encourage value analysis "on the fly" within the buyer's own plant. In a JIT plant, design engineers are not office-bound; they get out onto the shop floor, where they can work out small design changes with foremen.)

Mr. Claunch, Kawasaki's purchasing manager, relates one story of this type. A Minneapolis supplier of a part for the KLT three-wheeler had returned a bid that was high. "I tucked the prints under my arm," said Claunch, "flew to Minneapolis, and asked the engineers there 'Where are the dollars?' " They showed him where their high costs were, and without the need of going through Kawasaki engineers, Claunch was able to revise the specs to save supplier cost. The first bid was $17.65 per piece; the new bid was $12.00.

Focused Factories

As has been discussed, the potential advantages of supplier-buyer plant proximity apply in the United States as well as in Japan. Yet we see less of it in the States. The vastness of the country is one reason, but maybe not the main reason. Supplier proximity to buyer plants is especially common in the heavy-industry region around the Great Lakes and Ohio Valley. Independent machine shops and foundries abound, locating near to buyer plants that make farm machinery, autos, machine tools, and so forth. But the suppliers bid on work from the various buyers, and the competitive bidding environment is such that suppliers change often. Thus buyer-supplier plant relationships have tended to be precarious and standoffish.

Adding to the uncertainty is the threat that the buyer plant will decide to make something itself rather than buy it, thus leaving the supplier high and dry. For most of this century, U.S. industry considered vertical integration to be a desirable path to corporate growth and success. Ford's giant, vertically integrated River Rouge plant is a notable example. Wickham Skinner's 1974 article, "The Focused Factory,"[1] makes a strong case for the contrary path to success: development of special manufacturing competency in more narrowly focused areas. The focused factory is likely to be small and to resist vertical integration, i.e., expansion into the manufacture of parts previously supplied by other plants.

This, as it happens, is a favored strategy in many Japanese

industries, especially the automotive industry. For example, Toyota's expenditures for purchased materials account for nearly 80 percent of its sales dollar, whereas the figure is less than 50 percent for General Motors.[2] Toyota does, however, have an ownership interest in a number of its supplier companies.

A minority of Japanese manufacturers, including several prominent companies in cameras and electronics, follow the opposite strategy of extensive vertical integration. But on closer scrutiny, the strategies, as practiced in Japan, may not be quite so opposite as they seem at first glance. Toyota, Nissan, Honda, and many other companies that seem not to be vertically integrated actually exercise extensive control over their suppliers. Sometimes the supplier plants are partially owned by the buying firm. But even when that is not the case, control *is* exercised: Buyer representatives are constantly visiting the supplier plants and come to know the suppliers' capabilities and weaknesses, perhaps even better than a U.S. assembly plant typically knows its own subsidiary fabrication plants. On the other hand, Japanese companies that are highly vertically integrated in an ownership sense are often internally organized into small units, so that overcontrol does not stifle local initiative and pride. By small units, I mean small plants—most large Japanese corporations try to hold their plant size down to below 1,000 employees—and small, clearly identifiable work groups within each plant.

Thus, in Japan the real distinction between vertically integrated and focused corporations is not so great. But in the States our vertically integrated companies seem often to exercise smothering overcontrol while providing all too little real aid to wholly owned supplier plants. The focused-factory concept holds a good deal of appeal.

For companies that are not vertically integrated, the importance of purchasing is enhanced. Part of the Kawasaki training program in JIT buying is to emphasize the plant's long-term commitment to buying rather than making; Kawasaki wants to develop its final assembly competency and contract out as much fabrication as possible to fabrication experts. Such a commitment provides cement for strong, stable JIT agreements with reliable suppliers.

Probably few U.S. industrialists have read Skinner's article, but in recent years an increasing number of stories have appeared in the business press about companies that have retrenched—away from vertical integration. In the last few years U.S. executives have been exposed to news stories on the Japanese success phenomenon, including stories on the Japanese tendency to keep plants small and to rely heavily on extensive networks of suppliers. These events may encourage or signal some degree of nationwide withdrawal from vertical integration as a common, long-run corporate objective. If so, the climate for JIT buying will improve.

Sole-Source Purchasing

A rule of thumb in the U.S. purchasing trade is "Always have at least two suppliers for a given purchased part." Japanese companies, by contrast, hope to evolve to buying a given part from just one supplier—but a good one, and preferably one that does little business with other buyer companies; the Japanese buying firm wants to be the dominant reason for the supplier's existence. A supplier selling, say, 60 percent of its output to a single buying company will go to great lengths to be responsive.

In early 1981, the Kawasaki, Lincoln, plant was buying steel tubing from a distributor. The distributor sold for a number of far-flung tubing manufacturers, no one of which had an iota of commitment to be responsive to Kawasaki. Over the summer Kawasaki buyers, quality controllers, and design engineers worked with Brownie Manufacturing Co., a local company that had acquired used steel-tube-manufacturing equipment. Brownie gradually improved its quality and output, and in the fall Kawasaki negotiated a contract to buy about 30 percent of Brownie's

175

total output. From Brownie's point of view, the contract is large enough that it must heed Kawasaki's preferences for small, frequent deliveries and related services.

Price Competition in the United States

Building up and staying with a base of dedicated, high-quality suppliers—the Japanese way—seems resourceful, as compared with the supplier musical-chairs pattern that is practiced by many end-product manufacturers in the States. Our practice of frequent rebidding is supposedly justifiable in that it searches out the best current price. But that opens the door to those who would "buy in" low and then fail to perform satisfactorily. Also, in awarding a contract to a new lower bidder, you jerk the previous supplier off his learning curve and substitute a supplier who may have to go through a debugging period that the first supplier already experienced. Of course, the purchasing department is supposed to thoroughly check out a potential new supplier's capabilities before awarding a contract; but such investigation is time-consuming and subject to error—as compared with the administrative simplicity of sticking with the old supplier. Rebidding also fails to generate supplier loyalty, which can mean panic when the chips are down, i.e., when a supplier is unable to fill orders fast enough and must decide which buyer to favor.

The business and economic press in the United States has been telling us that in contrast to the Japanese, American managers are overly oriented toward short-term profits, at the expense of longer-term growth. The short-term-profit orientation would help explain why U.S. purchasing departments tend to place high priority on searching for the best price—which is done, of course, at the expense of building up a loyal supplier base. If U.S. industry responds to the criticism by shifting corporate emphasis toward the longer term, purchasing emphasis would shift accordingly, providing a healthy environment for JIT buying. But

176

even if the environment does not change, JIT buying could be attractive for many firms, because even in the short run, the combined costs—purchase price, paperwork, inventory carrying, transportation, and so on—may be less.

Will It Catch On?

JIT buying won't get very far very fast in this country if only Kawasaki and friends are pushing for it. There are, however, a few other U.S. plants that follow certain of the JIT buying practices. For example, Sony in San Diego has the Japanese instinct with regard to its suppliers. Sony has mostly local suppliers, with whom it hopes to "stay married for life." Sony, San Diego, is strictly an assembly plant and has no plans (or room) to vertically integrate, so suppliers need not worry about Sony initiating divorce proceedings without cause. Sony's QC people are at the suppliers' plants "all the time." Deliveries are to Sony's schedule, and delivery-quantity overages or underages are not tolerated.

At a Honda subsidiary plant in Marysville, Ohio (making motorcycles and beginning to manufacture autos), most parts come from Japan in boxed sets of 50—no more, no less. Mike Kreglow, the chief buyer, notes that at one meeting of Honda's purchasing staff, the Japanese purchasing managers asked for an explanation of the American practice of accepting delivery quantities when the overage or underage is up to 10 percent. The American buyers replied that they knew of no reason why, but that it was indeed common practice. The Japanese found this puzzling, and, needless to say, Honda will be trying to eliminate the overage/underage allowance in its dealings with U.S. suppliers. Other JIT practices that Kreglow sees as developing at Honda include seeking nearby suppliers and long-term relationships—"instead of re-quoting every year," as is the American practice. Perhaps the most significant JIT moves are with regard to freight. To gain better control, Honda recently began dealing with a contract trucking firm that will deliver direct from a key supplier to the Honda plant on Honda's schedule—as opposed to the former practice of relying on common carriers, who arranged loads and hauled at their own convenience. And for FOB-delivered goods, for which the supplier usually selects the shipping mode, Honda buyers sometimes try to intervene and designate the shipper.

And now some American-owned companies are beginning to implement just-in-time purchasing, especially U.S. automakers. In fact, the *Wall Street Journal* proclaimed just-in-time buying as the "latest craze" in Motor City.[3] The initial steps toward JIT buying involve the costliest parts: engines, axles, and transmissions. General Motors assembly plants had been receiving these kinds of parts according to calculations based on an average daily requirement, which did not always match up well with the plants' actual rates of usage. GM changed over to the type of system that Kawasaki and TRI-CON follow: tell the suppliers each morning how much to deliver and vary the quantities to match actual usage in the assembly plants.

There are a variety of obstacles to overcome. For example, one Buick assembly plant in Flint, Michigan, finds itself with many rail sidings and few truck-loading docks. Since JIT requires deliveries in small quantities, there is less need for rail car–sized deliveries, but trucks may arrive with small loads in such frequency as to swamp the truck docks.

Perhaps the greatest obstacles are numbers of parts options and numbers of suppliers. American automakers have gotten themselves into the option business to the extent that purchasers can custom-design the trimmings on the cars. Offering options seemed to yield marketing advantages that exceeded the small increases in labor cost. But the huge increases in inventories, and in production control and quality problems, tended to be overlooked. Now the enormity of these costs has been exposed through competition with the Japanese, and the U.S. auto companies must scale down their arrays of options.

Numbers of suppliers are also being cut back. GM vice-president Robert Stone states that about half the parts suppliers serving GM assembly plants are to be eliminated.[4] GM's fabrication plants, in turn, are seeking to reduce their numbers of steel suppliers.[5] GM will be picking as winners in this selection process the steelmakers with the highest-quality products, closest proximity to GM fabrication plants, and greatest commitment to remain steel producers—just what Japanese manufacturers look for in suppliers.

Industry Confederated

It should be clear from the chapter discussion that just-in-time purchasing brings about closer, friendlier, more mutually dependent relationships between companies doing business with each other. "The normal vendor-client relationship in the U.S. is adversarial and arm's-length," as *Fortune* magazine puts it.[6] But JIT purchasing interlinks companies into chains of suppliers and users, just as JIT production does for work centers within the plant. Each company is an island in the present U.S. system, but JIT purchasing would transform our manufacturing companies into "industry confederated." The benefits—higher productivity, better quality, and more stability—are unquestionably worth pursuing.

To sum up the chapter's simple and fundamental message, the seventh lesson may be restated as follows:

Have your suppliers deliver every day, or more often.

CHAPTER 8

Quality Circles, Work Improvement, and Specialization

LESSON 8: More self-improvement, fewer programs, less specialist intervention.

The quality control circle is a Japanese innovation, circa 1962, that formally mobilizes small voluntary teams of workers in order to improve quality and productivity. QC circles have been a magnet for the attention of Western visitors to Japan for nearly a decade. At first, the typical assessment was that "it won't work here." But beginning in 1974, a few Western companies—Lockheed in California was the first—tried QC circles and were pleased with the results.

In the early 1980s, quality circles (as they are called in the States) sprouted in Western industry, especially in North America, like dandelions in a spring lawn. The concept had caught the fancy of the organizational-behavior community in the business colleges and their practitioner counterparts in training and development posts in industry. "Circles" seemed to fit with what they had been advocating all along: worker participation and group dynamics.

The number of scholarly papers written in English on quality circles appears to be in the hundreds, and the number of Western companies that have instituted quality circle programs is in the hundreds of thousands. Quality circle consultants abound, and there is an International Association of Quality Circles. The quality circle concept is easy to understand and to implement, which partly explains why circles have become so popular.

The Impact of Quality Control Circles

In spite of all the Western enthusiasm for quality circles (and their wide use in Japan), Japanese subsidiary plants in the West generally have not implemented them. The number of Japanese plants in this country is in the hundreds, but few, if any, have quality control circles.

It appears that for the Japanese, circles are way down on a priority-ordered list of important things to get accomplished—and this may apply to plants in Japan as well as in other countries. Hayes notes that "most of the [Japanese] companies I talked to already had enviable reputations for high-quality products by the time they adopted QCs."[1] Nor are quality control circles universally popular among top Japanese companies. Seiuemon Inaba, president of Fujitsu Fanuc, a premier robot manufacturer, told a group of visiting dignitaries, including U.S. senators: The QC circle "system is ritualistic" and unlikely to produce much in the way of useful suggestions.[2]

Quality control circles may have only a modest impact, because, as Junji Noguchi, general manager of the Union of Japanese Scientists and Engineers, puts it, "Workers and foremen can solve only 15 percent of all quality control problems. The rest must be handled by management or the engineering staff."[3] Juran echoes the point, only more emphatically: "There is no possibility for the workforce to make a major contribution to solving a company's quality problems."[4] He explains further that quality control circles (which he favors for their human relations benefits) can deal with the "trivial many," that is, the small problems, but major quality matters are related to vendor relations, management policies, process designs, and other areas outside the workers' sphere of influence. Robert Cole, long a leading U.S. authority on the Japanese work culture, observes that "few [U.S.] companies have had the circles in operation for more than two years" and "it would be premature to make assessments as to their suitability to the American environment."[5]

Most of the Japanese plants that I have visited have vigorous QC circle programs, and I am personally impressed by their apparent contributions to quality improvement, to methods improvement, to morale-enhancing improvements, and to worker motivation. Also I believe that in some Japanese companies QC circles played an important role early in the history of the Japanese quality control movement. The early role that I refer to has to do with the training of workers in quality control concepts and techniques in the 1960s. The Japanese periodical *Gemba To QC* (Quality Control for Foremen) began publication in 1962, and according to one report, the "QC circle was originally formed as a study group at workshop level, using the magazine as a textbook."[6]

Undoubtedly many of those QC circles of the 1960s era began making helpful contributions and have continued doing so year after year. In many other Japanese companies, QC circles were formed much later, and not for training purposes so much as for purposes of solving problems and generating ideas.

A third way that QC circles form is of their own accord—the natural tendency of people with a common interest to band together. One impetus for the natural formation of informal groups of workers who care to discuss common work-related issues is minimal inventory buffers. As was explained in Chapter 2, when the inventory barricades between workers come down, their tasks become more closely linked; they have collective work-related problems to talk about in their spare time.

The inherent good sense of employee involvement—of just about any kind—suggests that the many Western companies that have jumped on the quality circle bandwagon will surely benefit from doing so. Quality circle implementers should not, however, expect these benefits to amount to significant improvements in quality control. QC circles are very evident in Japanese plants today, but primarily as a way of wringing the last defects out of a production system that has already achieved outstanding quality. Years of training and plant-wide efforts in accordance with the total quality control (TQC) concepts discussed in Chapter 3 were the means by which Japan's cycle of rapid and continual quality improvement was created. In sum, it is a mistake to think of QC circles—for all their morale and motivation advantages—as a ticket to achieving the quality levels that have been attained by the Japanese. In fact, QC circles founded on such a premise could do more harm than good in that they might delay for several years the introduction of a real quality control program.

Are QC Circles Like Other Western Work Improvement Programs?

With the introduction of almost any management program, some doubting Thomases will say, "We tried this before, only it was called. . . ." And so it is with quality circles. In each of the many U.S. companies that have adopted a quality circle program, some employees undoubtedly view it as another addition to a long line of work improvement programs tried by the company over the years. Some old-timers are likely to claim that quality circles are "just the same as our old work simplification program"; some may even assert that circles are the same as their old zero defects program or their current employee suggestions program.

Other Programs

Quality circles are not the same as work simplification—nor are they identical with either zero defects or employee suggestions programs. But the resemblances are close. There are a few other work improvement programs that overlap with quality circles to a notable extent: value engineering/value analysis, industrial engineering/work study, and quality assurance/quality control, each of which exists as a permanent organizational unit in many companies. Quality circles also relate to other organization-wide programs such as quality of work life, Scanlon plans, and organizational development.

The nature of the similarities among all these programs is important to our understanding of the Western vs. the Japanese approach to work improvement and employee involvement. Table 8–1 summarizes some of the key similarities—in approach and in objectives—among ten related work-improvement programs, and each program is separately discussed below.

QC Circles

The quality control circle, listed first in Table 8–1, is a small, formally organized group of workers. The agenda and procedures of a quality control circle are usually quite structured, but the details vary somewhat from firm to firm, depending upon the objectives that are being emphasized. For example, methods analysis charting procedures may be used if methods improvement goals are foremost; and fishbone charts may be developed to improve quality. Methods and quality objectives are generally important in Japanese quality control circles but are sometimes not emphasized in U.S.circles. In both Japan and the States, morale-enhancing ideas—softball leagues, vending machines, repainting the lunchroom, and so on—are legitimate topics for QC circle discussion, and motivational benefits are expected to derive from the employee participation that takes place in circles.

185

TABLE 8–1. Work Improvement Programs

Program name	IMPROVEMENT APPROACH					OBJECTIVES				
	Worker involvement	Specialist-oriented	Group	Individual	Procedural	Work methods	Quality	Product design	Morale-enhancing changes	Motivation
Quality circles	✓		✓		✓	✓	✓		✓	✓
Zero defects	✓			✓			✓			
Employee suggestions	✓			✓		✓	✓	✓	✓	✓
Work simplification	✓		✓		✓	✓				✓
Quality of work life	✓		✓			✓	✓	✓	✓	✓
Scanlon plan	✓		✓			✓				✓
VE/VA		✓	✓		✓			✓		
IE/work study		✓		✓	✓	✓				
QA/QC		✓		✓	✓		✓			
Organizational development	✓	✓	✓	✓	✓				✓	✓

Indeed morale and motivation are frequently stated as the main objectives in this country, and sometimes in Japan as well.

Before discussing the other nine programs in Table 8–1, I should point out a basic difference in attitude with regard to such programs. In the United States, we are "program-happy." We tend to build a formal program, and maybe a whole new staff organization to administer it, whenever a promising management concept comes along. Our attitude seems to be: The more management programs, the better. Some Japanese companies may be that way, but most seem more inclined toward an opposite attitude: The fewer programs (and staff positions to run them), the better.

It is true that Japan has gone mad over QC circles, and Japanese QC circles have become highly organized and institutionalized nationwide. But in Japan the QC circle is not the program; total quality control is. Or, more properly, TQC is a fundamental production function, and QC circles, plus the 19 other concepts of TQC presented in Chapter 3, are means of performing that function.

The worker involvement–oriented programs discussed next are very Western and not very Japanese. Japanese plants with QC circles already have worker involvement, and why duplicate?

Western Worker-Involvement Programs

The next five programs in Table 8–1, like QC circles, feature worker involvement: zero defects, employee suggestions, work simplification, quality of work life, and Scanlon plans. Each program differs from QC circles in certain other respects.

Zero Defects

Zero defects (ZD) *sounds* similar to quality control circles. Actually ZD and QC circles are quite different in approach. As the check marks in Table 8–1 show, ZD generates ideas (entered on "error cause removal" forms) from workers as individuals, but QC circles rely on worker groups for ideas. There are no special procedures followed in ZD idea generation, but QC circles usually do follow a step-by-step procedure. ZD objectives are limited to quality improvement ideas, whereas QC circles are aimed at quality, methods, morale, and motivation objectives.

Some might argue that since ZD involves workers, there are motivational advantages. My impression is that ZD does not result in motivation so much as it *relies* on motivation. ZD seems to have enjoyed its greatest success in its early developmental years in the U.S. aerospace industry. The time was the early 1960s, when the United States was worried about its "missile gap" vis-à-vis the Soviet Union. Patriotic feelings ran high, and patriotic motivation made it easy for workers to accept the zero defects imperative.

I must point out that the Japanese use the term *zero defects* a good deal. "Zero defects" aptly conveys the fundamental goal of perfection. Since, in the United States, "zero defects" is often identified with formal ZD programs, I am using the term *perfection,* rather than ZD, to express the basic goal of Japanese TQC systems.

Employee Suggestions

Employee suggestions programs are very common in U.S. industry but less so in Japan. Employee suggestions are individually generated, and no special procedures for innovation are followed. Suggestions programs have all the objectives of QC circles, plus one more: improvement of product design. Employee suggestions generally provide cash awards, which, along with the chance to participate, improve motivation.

In Japanese companies that I have visited, individual employee suggestions are welcomed, and they constitute a creditable portion of the work improvement projects. Thus, group

188

endeavor is not somehow thought of as "the Japanese way" and treated as an end in itself. Rather, the reason why group activities seem so much in evidence to Western visitors is the group orientation that is naturally associated with project-by-project improvement. The plant management staff approves proposals for improvement projects and assigns them to *those* most concerned —plural—because work improvement nearly always affects several people.

Work Simplification

In a work simplification program, supervisors and workers are taught how to conduct systematic methods studies through the use of process flow charts, left-and-right-hand charts, man-machine charts, principles of motion economy, and so forth. So trained, the line workers may study and improve their own tasks, as opposed to being studied by analysts from industrial engineering. Work simplification programs, a U.S. innovation, had their heyday in about the 1940s. The war production effort provided impetus for methods improvement, and scarcities of industrial engineers provided the rationale for involving groups from the production centers in work study. Work simplification is gone and forgotten in most companies today. (A few programs still exist: for example, a longstanding work simplification program at the Dynamatic Division of Eaton Corp.) But work simplification warrants our attention since it is the program most nearly like QC circles. As the check marks in Table 8–1 show, the improvement approaches followed in the two programs feature the same key characteristics: worker involvement, group orientation, and a structured modus operandi. (In both cases the step-by-step procedures follow the scientific method of inquiry, but the details and study aids differ.) The main differences are in objectives. Work simplification is limited to study of work methods, not quality or morale-enhancing improvements.

189

Quality of Work Life

Quality of work life (QWL) is new, and I include it simply because it is widely discussed today as a quality circle-like program. General Motors coined the name, and today QWL has counterparts in a number of other industrial companies. QWL programs are still too new to categorize precisely, but in general the programs are oriented toward worker involvement and group analysis—so far without a stable step-by-step procedural approach. The objectives of QWL seem broad, emphasizing morale-enhancing changes and motivation, but also sometimes including work methods, quality, and product design.

Scanlon Plans

Scanlon plans involve workers acting in groups (not following any set procedure) to cut costs, and savings are passed on to the workers as a whole. Joseph N. Scanlon's idea was popular in business college classrooms when I was a graduate student (in the 1960s), but since then I hadn't heard much about it until recently. The Japanese productivity challenge seems to have triggered renewed interest in Scanlon plans, which focus on work methods, not on quality, product design, or morale-enhancing ideas. The cash payout to employees, plus the chance to participate, improves motivation.

Programs Featuring Specialist Intervention

I have never been personally comfortable in the various jobs I have held as a specialist (including management consulting). The specialist's job is to introduce special expertise when the situation warrants it—or, to use a term in vogue among organizational behaviorists, when an "intervention" is needed. An intervention is an encroachment by an outsider (usually a highly paid outsider) who can easily walk away and hide after intervening.

The obvious deficiencies in a system relying heavily on specialist intervention lead most of us, I think, to intellectually prefer the nonspecialist ways of doing the same things. That is, we tend to prefer the first six work improvement programs in Table 8–1, which get the workers to generate their own improvements rather than being subject to outside intervention.

But though our heads and our hearts may be on the side of employee involvement, our egos and our pocketbooks often favor specialist involvement. We who are highly educated in a specialty of some kind receive ego gratification from being called upon to provide expert advice. Pocketbooks swell as well as heads, since expert advice commands a high price. Japanese specialists are the same, but (1) there aren't so many of them, (2) they don't operate in a freewheeling specialist-oriented environment, and (3) many are hired into general supervisory line positions rather than staff specialist positions.

There are four staff specialties that are particularly relevant to this discussion of programs similar to quality control circles: value engineering/value analysis (VA/VE); industrial engineering (IE)/work study; quality assurance/quality control (QA/QC); and organizational development. Each is considered below.

Value Engineering/Value Analysis

Value analysis (VA), developed in the purchasing department of General Electric Co. in 1947, is a procedure for analyzing product designs in order to improve value (cut cost). Value analysis is known as value engineering (VE) in organizations in which the procedure has been taken over by product design engineers. The VA/VE procedure is formal and systematic, and one step in the procedure, an idea-generation method known as brainstorming, is also one of the steps followed in QC circle investigations. VA/VE also resembles QC circles in that both feature group analysis. There the similarity ends: VA/VE is a function of specialists, not workers, and VA/VE has product design as its only objective, which is the one objective listed in Table 8–1 that is *not* pursued in QC circle programs. Thus VA/VE might be considered more as complementary to QC circles than as an alternative program.

This comparison of VA/VE with QC circles is supplementary to earlier mention of how value analysis ties in with just-in-time purchasing (Chapter 7). That discussion may have understated the popularity of value analysis in Japanese industry, both in design engineering and purchasing. But there it is popular as an engineering and purchasing technique rather than as a formal program run by a VA/VE coordinator, or, as in some U.S. companies and defense agencies, a separate staff department.

Industrial Engineering/Work Study

Industrial engineering is a profession that, among other things, conducts work studies to improve work methods. Some of the procedures of work study, such as process flow charts, are found in the repertoire of tools used by QC circles. The IE/work study approach employs specialists working as individuals, which is contrary to the worker-group orientation of QC circles. As Table 8–1 indicates, the objectives of IE/work study and QC circles are mostly different, work methods being the only objective the two have in common.

But focusing on the dissimilarities paints a false picture. As discussion in previous chapters has pointed out, industrial engineering is highly esteemed in Japanese industry. In the Toyota family of companies, IE degrees are pursued and attained by many production foremen. In other Japanese companies, IE is the only specialty that exists as a sizeable staff department. And in most Japanese companies, IE/work study concepts are influential from the ′op to the bottom of the organization.

In those companies where industrial engineers are in a separate IE department, they are very unlikely to be desk-bound, as is often the case in Western industry. Instead the industrial engineer is likely to be the right-hand man of a foreman (rather like a dispatcher is to a foreman in so many Western job shops) or an active resource person for QC circles and similar worker groups. Among foremen and worker groups, project-by-project improvement of quality goes on continually, and in many of the projects improvements in quality and work methods go together; IEs are frequently called in to help with process design, tooling improvement, relayout of facilities, time studies, and so forth.

I have been astounded by statements I have heard from some American "authorities" to the effect that the Japanese reject Taylorism, supposedly in favor of a more humanistic approach. Frederick W. Taylor, an American, is the father of IE/work study, circa 1900, but the Japanese out-Taylor us all—including putting Taylor to good use in QC circles or small group improvement activities.

Quality Assurance/Quality Control

What has just been said about IE/work study applies also to QA/QC, except that QA/QC has a quality rather than a work methods objective. That is, QA/QC shares one objective (quality) as well as some procedures (e.g., statistical quality control charting) with QC circles, but Western QA/QC employs individual analysis by specialists, not group study by workers. In total quality control, as was noted in Chapter 3, the Japanese QA/QC people are likely to be few, since production has the primary responsibility for quality.

193

Organizational Development

Organizational development (OD), the final entry in Table 8–1, has become a recognized specialty in the United States, though not to the point where companies are likely to have a permanent OD department. Instead, OD is usually a program. OD differs from the other nine programs in Table 8–1 in that it is both specialist- and worker-oriented. OD specialists, as individuals, meet with worker groups to try to bring about change. Formal procedures are often followed in developing the prescriptions for change. While the organizational development *approach* is broader than that of QC circles, OD *objectives* are narrower, being limited to morale-enhancing changes and motivation gained by worker involvement. An OD article of faith is that the morale and motivation enhancements will lead to higher productivity, but, of course, there may be technological (methods, equipment, resource delivery) obstacles in the way. OD specialists employ an extensive kit of social-psychological tools—virtually anything that seems to work—and in the United States, where OD is especially popular, it appears that OD people are treating QC circles as one more "intervention strategy."

Combating Specialization

The subject just discussed, the Western penchant to "staff off" basic functions to specialists, is worth following through, because there is growing agreement that staff specialization is a critical obstacle to improvement. The specialization problem may be looked at in two ways. One is the lack of job rotation, which prevents specialists from ever acquiring a broad, company-wide outlook. The other is that there are simply too many such people. Here are a few of the critics who are spreading these messages:

194

Ouchi: "In the United States we conduct our careers between organizations but within a single specialty. In Japan people conduct careers between specialties but within a single organization."[7]

Drucker: "The unchecked growth and excessive power of service staffs is considered by practically all our foreign critics to be a serious weakness of U.S. industry, and a major cause of its poor performance."[8]

Patton: "[One reason] why Japan has been able to invade U.S. markets successfully in one industry after another [is that in the U.S.] staff positions have far outstripped line jobs in number and in influence."[9]

Zealous application of the job rotation concept is the norm in Japanese industry. Job rotation is pursued with special brilliance at Mitsubishi Electric Corp., a leading Japanese manufacturer of electric machinery. Sadakazu Shindo, the president of Mitsubishi, explains how even the technical people are included, in spite of a common belief that "rotations in technical experts [are] to be avoided not only for the corporation but also for the personnel involved."[10] Shindo firmly believes that job rotation of technical people is necessary in order to spread technology around the corporation (that is, to effect technological transfer). Some examples of Mitsubishi's rotations are: electronic experts in manufacturing and specialists in heavy electric machinery going to research institutes and then to home electric appliances; and mass production experts in home electric appliances transferring to electronics sectors, via the research institutes. Mitsubishi set up its research institutes many years ago, and they have served as a hub for job rotation as well as performing their primary function of conducting developmental research. Recently a special headquarters group was created to further promote technological transfer and job rotation of experts.

Similar attention to job rotation—of experts and nonexperts as well—is sorely needed in U.S. industry. Some U.S. companies are already trying to do something about the staff burden. Ford executives believe that their salaried-staff costs, estimated at $4 billion a year, are twice that of Japanese automakers; Ford made a dent in the problem by reducing staff by 26 percent in 1979–1981.[11]

A small number of U.S. executives have resisted the nationwide tendency in the last 20 or 25 years to give free rein to growth of staff departments and staff-controlled improvement programs; to put the most talented new employees into staff jobs, and keep them there; and to load executive suites with people who have no line experience (that is, none in production or direct production-support functions like production control, materials management, and engineering). For example, some years ago Cornell Maier, president of Kaiser Aluminum and Chemical Corp., stated: "The only things you really need to run a business are materials, machines, workers, and salesmen. Nobody else is justified unless he's helping the worker produce more product or the salesman sell more product."[12]

An example of a U.S. executive who dramatically resolved a company's specialist problem is now a part of American management folklore. The executive was Robert Townsend, and the year was 1963. Townsend has written about how he became president of money-losing Avis, the rent-a-car company, and set about to rescue the firm. Avis managers gave Townsend a wide range of excuses for the failure of their departments to meet performance targets, and many of the reasons had to do with not being able to purchase the materials and hire the people they needed—because of red tape in the purchasing and personnel departments. Townsend's solution: Fire the purchasing and personnel departments, and let the line department heads do their own buying and hiring. Townsend's little book, a management "A to Z" treatise, probably seems simplistic to most management scholars. But the book contains a lesson in transforming an overspecialized company into more of a Japanese-style organization in which line managers have a full measure of responsibility for their departments' performance.[13]

I have been clipping stories about people like Maier and Townsend for years, and I have been preaching the same viewpoint in my classroom[14]—largely to deaf ears, I suppose, until recent years, when the Japanese story became available to lend support. I have been struck over the years not only by growth of staff but also by the way that company after American company has been letting its job rotation fall by the wayside. At the time of my graduation from engineering school (1961), job rotation was a buzzword among those of us going through job interviews. *Don't* ask about the company's retirement program, we advised each other; *do* ask about its job rotation program. Today's graduates "dress for success" instead.

A Lesson to Be Relearned

Of all the lessons in this book, the eighth is the one that best qualifies as relearning. In an earlier era, Western industry was lean and hungry. In the 1950s, it prospered and ate fatty foods, and now it is suffering from hardening of the arteries. The fat is nonproductive staff, which not only is expensive but actually is an obstacle to fast response and the pursuit of actions done for the good of the *whole* organization.

The Japanese have also prospered but have not gotten fat. My roundabout explanation for this is that the Japanese environment of scarcity and overcrowding has discouraged profligate habits and encouraged only those techniques that prevent waste —especially the just-in-time system and total quality control. The wastefulness of staff growth and overspecialization is not to be tolerated any more than inventory buildup and the waste of producing defective parts.

The Japanese have not discovered anything new nor amended any of the old lessons regarding line and staff people. They have simply stuck with the natural state of helping line managers and workers to improve themselves in order to do their own jobs better. Line people thus are given training and education so that *they* are the experts, job rotation so that *they* have the perspective to make major decisions, and staff support when *they* request it. We know how to do all of these things. We need only to get back to doing them.

The lesson of this chapter, lesson 8, may now be restated:

Industry does not need a lot of improvement programs coordinated or run by specialists; production managers and workers can do it themselves.

CHAPTER 9

Prospects for Catching Up

LESSON 9: Simplicity is the natural state.

Can the Japanese production system be made to work in the United States and other Western industrialized countries? I have been answering yes to the question all through the book. In several respects the muddle that Western industry finds itself in is similar to the situation Japan was in when it embarked upon its great postwar quality crusade. Specifically, there seem to have been five situational factors that led to Japan's success in overcoming its severe quality problem; the same five factors are present in Western industry and are likely to drive the West toward a closing of the quality and productivity gap vis-à-vis the Japanese. In this chapter we examine the Western prospects for catching up, and briefly examine potential applications of JIT/TQC in developing and underdeveloped countries as well.

Why We Will Catch Up

The five factors lending impetus to a drive for change and improvement in Western industry are as follows:

1. *Awareness that there is a gap*. Japan was acutely aware, in the post–World War II recovery period, that the world considered "Made in Japan" to mean "made poorly." Clearly Western industry today is aware of the quality and productivity advantage enjoyed by Japanese export industries. This is especially true in the U.S. auto industry, which in the past year became thoroughly aroused by the "Harbour report." Jim Harbour, a consultant and former director of corporate manufacturing engineering at Chrysler, conducted studies comparing costs to produce an automobile in the United States and Japan. (One study report is available from the U.S. Department of Transportation, Transportation Systems Center, Contract DTRS–57–81–C–00036, submitted by James E. Harbour.) Harbour's conclusion—that the Japanese can manufacture a compact car for $1,600 less than a U.S. auto company—is consistent with other reports. What is dramatic about the Harbour report is its careful documentation of the components of that cost difference, most of which are traceable to Japan's just-in-time production system. Harbour shows large JIT-based savings on inventory, on space, on avoidance of defectives, and so forth.

2. *Determination to improve*. Japan was a strong, proud industrialized nation prior to its defeat in World War II, and, like Europe, was determined to recover and rebuild following the war. The United States has suffered enough plant shutdowns and losses of whole industries because of inability to compete; the resulting social and economic upheavals and stinging losses of prestige have fostered a national resolve to make changes.

3. *Belief that change is possible*. A few years ago, Western

200

industry reacted to Japan's successes with much moaning about Japan's wage advantage, supportive government, and alleged dumping activities (selling below cost in export markets). Today the United States is bristling with more positive activities: Ford's quality campaign, GM's just-in-time purchasing efforts, consultants crisscrossing the country marketing their views on how to catch up with the Japanese, management development programs on Japanese techniques in every city. The activities show a new "can do" spirit.

An aggressive, literate, achievement-oriented society is unlikely to remain negative about itself for long. Japan didn't after World War II, and the United States did not continue its hand wringing for very long following its recent discovery of the quality/productivity gap vis-à-vis Japan. American companies sent delegations to Japan to learn, they learned enough to get started, and the catch-up era has begun.

Popular 1981 books by Ouchi[1] and by Pascale and Athos[2] helped industry to adopt a positive mood. They pointed out that some of the best U.S. companies, on their own, developed certain broad management practices observable in many Japanese companies. Their message is that obviously we can do it, because we already have.

4. *Know-how.* Those early books (if less than two years old may be called early) were published before much was known in the West about Japanese techniques. Indeed, at that time it was popular to presume that Japanese success has little to do with *techniques.* Since this book is literally brimming with Japanese techniques—those included in the multifaceted, elaborately simple, and highly effective JIT/TQC system—one can safely reject that notion.

The Japanese got started on their quality crusade by acquiring quality control know-how from such American experts as Deming and Juran. We, in turn, are acquiring our know-how today from the Japanese. We half-believe we can do it when we see it done in Japan. And when we see a full range of just-in-time

201

techniques in operation with U.S. workers (e.g., at Kawasaki, Nebraska) and a host of total quality control concepts and techniques in force in U.S. electronics plants (e.g., Sony's, Sanyo's, and Matsushita's U.S. subsidiaries), we must know that our culture is no obstacle.

5. *Timing.* When things are going well, it is hard to find the time or the will to change. Japan's quality campaign began when things were not going well, i.e., when the country was recovering and rebuilding after World War II. The U.S. recession of 1981–1982 hardly compares; still, a recession does bring on self-examination, and frequently change. Furthermore, during a recession most companies have excess staff who can be assigned to projects geared for change. Probably most U.S. companies do not yet know enough about the Japanese JIT/TQC system to seize this opportunity to start their own JIT/TQC campaign. But a few have done so.

For example, Rolm Corp., a California electronics manufacturer, sent a delegation to a seminar in Lincoln, Nebraska, on Japanese techniques at which I was a speaker. (The seminar included a tour of the Kawasaki, Lincoln, facility.) The delegation told me that Rolm had been growing so fast there was no time to do any more than "get the product out." When the growth rate slowed down in the 1981 recession, Rolm executives found the time to go to Japan and tour Japanese plants. They returned enthusiastic about initiating their own just-in-time system, and the company pulled three key plant management people off their jobs to constitute their JIT project group; this group came to the Lincoln seminar to learn what they could about how to proceed.*

---

* In Rolm's case the recession afforded an opportunity to initiate JIT. Just-in-time had its beginnings at Toyota not in a mere recession but in a genuine corporate crisis. Toyota was in danger of bankruptcy, and the entire work force was aware of it. According to Taiichi Ohno, a Toyota vice-president and one of the JIT architects, the necessary cooperation of the Toyota work force could not have been secured without the feelings of panic over possible bankruptcy. (Since I have been unable to obtain English translations of Ohno's articles and books, I am relying on Japanese friends who have read them for these statements.)

202

There are a fair number of other U.S. companies that, like Rolm, have started a JIT/TQC project. They will find out what implementation procedures work best, and before the decade is over, JIT and TQC should be widespread in American and other Western industry.

Institutional Factors

Much has been said in the press about institutional and structural differences between Japan and the United States: for example, differences related to personal savings, private investment, types of labor unions, employee mobility between companies, technical literacy, antitrust laws, and government-industry cooperation. While I tend to agree with many of the popular suggestions regarding changes in our American institutions, I believe that these issues are complex and that their resolution is far less sure to get good results than is the more direct path to catching up with the Japanese, i.e., adoption of their *techniques*. One problem is that many of the complex institutional issues are two-sided. A few examples will illustrate.

Tax Laws

For example, if our tax laws favored higher family savings to generate more capital for plant investment, our plants might spend the money on:

1. Conveyors, which the Japanese have shown are sometimes counterproductive (see Chapters 4 and 5).

2. Automated storage facilities (e.g., stacker cranes), which store costly inventory rather than eliminate it (see Chapter 5).

3. "Super machines," which hamper flexibility; take too much time to set up; require high utilization to amortize, which tends to mean that parts are made whether needed or not; and cost too much, as compared with Japanese-style, self-developed, lightweight, special-purpose machines (see Chapter 6).

4. Robots, which Japan, with its extremely low birthrate, needs more than we do, with our steady influx of new labor through legal and illegal immigration.

Some sectors of industry need a lot of capital. The steel industry and all other capital-intensive processing industries cannot compete with the Japanese for long if they do not spend a good deal on modernization. But a shortage of capital does not seem to be the big problem in most of the durable finished-goods industries.

"Japan, Inc."

A second two-sided issue is government-industry cooperation. The Japanese Ministry of International Trade and Industry (MITI) has some power (money) to nurture industries that look like winners and to discourage industries that look like losers. The Western press—and some Western authorities who should know better—have seized upon Japan's brand of national economic planning as somehow being a vital key to Japan's industrial strength. I would tend to agree that MITI has for the most part done a decent job of picking winners and losers. But judging from the sad performance of national economic planners in Eastern Europe, Cuba, and other socialist or communist regions, and the mediocre performance of planners in various Western European countries, especially France, I see no reason to believe that MITI is at all immune to horrendous mistakes.

Errors have already been made. One that has been publicized is MITI's abortive effort to convince Japan's auto industry to retrench.[3] It appeared to MITI that Japan's industry would not long be able to compete internationally with growing automotive industries in such low-wage countries as Brazil and Malaysia. MITI's error in that instance was of no consequence, because the six Japanese automakers (Toyota, Nissan, Honda, Isuzu, Mitsubishi, and Tōyō Kōgyō) ignored MITI and proceeded to thrive. Where did MITI go wrong? For one thing, no group of government planners can predict change; all they can do is react to what they know about the past and present. MITI planners could not know that Toyota would develop the just-in-time production system, which may be the most important productivity-enhancing management innovation since Taylor's scientific management at the turn of the century. All the Japanese auto companies now have their own vigorous JIT programs, and American automakers are beginning to implement JIT as well.

What if the United States had had a MITI-like organization over the last two or three decades? Probably such poor performers as the textile and the shoe industries would have been ridiculed and beaten down even more rapidly than they were under international competition. Yet *The Wall Street Journal* tells us that American shoe manufacturers recently "have invested heavily in new technology and can keep pace with, and sometimes outstrip, European and Japanese competitors." And, "In the early 1970s," the textile industry "was a classic case of how the U.S. had lost competitiveness. . . . Over the last 10 years, however, the industry has undergone a major streamlining and modernization that has made U.S. textile manufacturers competitive again."[4]

If one were an economic planner, Japan would be a better than average place to practice. The Japanese islands are quite insulated and isolated demographically, so that one can predict the future work force, by age group and education level, rather accurately; and stable, crowded, resource-poor Japan does not

205

undergo massive internal migrations in the quest for gold, crude oil, sunshine, Rocky Mountains energy, and so forth. The heterogeneous, vast, uncrowded, resource-rich, dynamic North American continent is, by comparison, a planner's nightmare. The growth and decline of specific industries is hardly predictable. It would seem that North America will continue to specialize in not a few types of industries but nearly all types: high tech/ low tech, labor-intensive/capital-intensive, agricultural/industrial, automated/manual, skilled craftsmanship/grunt labor, services/goods, energy-yielding/energy-consuming. It seems pointless to interfere with entrepreneurial processes by setting up national commissions to carry out the futile task of trying to separate stars from dogs—an exercise likely to benefit no one but lobbyists.

Lifetime Employment

One more two-sided institutional (or structural) factor is labor mobility. The Japanese tradition of lifetime employment (in major companies) nurtures dedicated employees. America's own IBM Corp. is the same way. We are told that our company-hopping ways (aside from IBM and a few other exceptions) doom us to an uncommitted work force, discontinuity, and frequent cases of projects started but not completed. These deficiencies are quite real, but the Japanese system has its problems, too. Yuzaburo Mogi, first executive vice-president of Kikkoman Foods, Inc., in Walworth, Wisconsin, and general manager of Kikkoman International, says of the Japanese seniority system: "While it offers security and creates a more harmonious atmosphere conducive to good results, it may also reduce incentives to do good work."[5]

Sadakazu Shindo, chairman of the giant-sized Mitsubishi Electric Co., makes a related point: "I believe that 'right men in the right places' remains . . . the best single principle in motivating the workers to do their best. Enthusiasm to work can result

206

only when employees are located in the places where they themselves wanted to be in the first place."[6] With this statement Shindo might be advocating American-style labor mobility: people moving about from job to job, career to career, and company to company in the quest for a fulfilling position that they can be enthusiastic about. But, of course, Shindo is advocating no such thing. Mitsubishi employees are Mitsubishi employees for life. What Shindo is explaining is the need for careful employee selection, evaluation, and placement into positions that will maximize their happiness and potential. In the Japanese system this puts a great burden on management, who must perform the selections, evaluations, and placements. Western managers have the same difficult task to perform, but when they do it badly, the employee quits and finds another job in another organization. Shindo is a remarkable executive who has created procedures and organizational units specifically for employee mobility *within* Mitsubishi; still, Mitsubishi's system relies heavily on managerial judgment, and managers are fallible. The Western employee at least has a handy escape valve: resignation.

Other structural factors similarly could be discussed as two-sided issues, but perhaps it is unnecessary to go on. The point is simply that structural factors are complex, and structural solutions are often debatable. The safe course of action is to concentrate improvement efforts on proven techniques, and the Japanese indeed have an abundance of proven JIT/TQC techniques to offer.

The Natural State

Part of the reason that American industrialists, politicians, economists, and others have advocated laws and regulations more favorable to industry is the impression that our industries have become poor and backward in comparison with their Japanese

207

counterparts. The common belief is that our industries are deprived and therefore need *more* of whatever money can buy. Actually, the JIT/TQC message is that we should try to get by with *less*: less setup time, less inventory, less inspection, less control, less paperwork and computing, less elaborate equipment, less specialization.

In some respects, the worker in a JIT/TQC environment is like the craftsman of the simple pre-factory era. The skill levels are not comparable, but there are these similarities: The JIT/TQC worker, like the craftsman, makes one piece at a time (ideally). The craftsman (or JIT/TQC worker) and his customers (or neighboring workers) examine the results right away. Errors surface before many more are produced, and they receive immediate and direct attention. And for both craftsman and JIT/TQC worker, it is natural to rethink what you (or you and your work group) did today and how you can do better tomorrow.

Growing Complex

Manufacturing companies always start out lean and simple: a small number of managers with broad responsibilities and job rotation by necessity; flexible production workers who perform multiple jobs and check their own work; simple self-developed equipment; no separation into self-contained job shops; hand-to-mouth, in-plant inventory control; minimal shop paper; no interference by staff specialists. As the company grows—in physical size, number of employees, number of products and models, and number of markets—all this changes. Coordination becomes difficult, so we add coordinators, controls, forms, reports, and inventory buffers. If we receive a large order, we acquire a few large machines, which are so expensive that we feel compelled to run them day and night, turning out parts that will be held in inventory until sales can find buyers for them. The machines are organized first into machine centers, then into separate job shops;

and elaborate information systems are added to control flows between shops. We are afraid that manufacturing will be too busy producing to worry about quality, processes, methods, maintenance, provisioning, training, safety, scheduling, and so forth. So we hire staff experts to perform each of these functions. But the experts get in one another's way, they pursue self-serving objectives, they add heavy-handed controls, their numbers grow, and they spend money.

When all of this gets out of hand and the company is generating red ink, company officials lay off people and slash budgets. The company usually survives and may go through several cycles like this before it finally fails, or is acquired in order to avoid failure.

What our companies need is a way to grow and obtain economies of scale without all of the dis-economies of scale, namely, layers of costly staff and complex controls. In short, we need ways to stay simple. And Japanese industry provides what we seek. The Japanese environment has served as the world's Petri dish from which a new industrial culture of simplicity has grown. We should not be surprised to find that the simple JIT and TQC concepts that constitute the emergent culture are familiar to us, because they resemble what went on in our own companies when they were small. This is a pleasant thing to discover, because we know we can do what we have done before. The natural state is not forbidding.

Nonindustrialized Countries

It is clear that Western industry is badly in need of the sort of revitalization that JIT/TQC simplicity affords. Just-in-time/total quality control also holds appeal to developing countries (those with oil) and underdeveloped countries (those without oil). Oil money has been paying for masses of bright young people to attend Western colleges so that they may return to their developing countries and help build an industrial base for the time when the oil is gone. They may learn too much about too little and go home eager to become revered experts in risk management or automated storage and retrieval, settling into lifetime specialty careers as they see their Western role models doing. In this scenario, the best minds are working out complicated solutions to narrow problems. One wonders how the plants built with oil money will ever be competitive in world markets.

The JIT/TQC approach seems particularly fitting in underdeveloped countries. They have the advantage of very low labor costs and no problem about too much specialization and complicated solutions. JIT/TQC is a natural for the kinds of labor-intensive manufacturing that generally begin in these countries. The investors are often foreign companies building subsidiaries where labor is cheap, and they have a golden opportunity to make these subsidiaries showcases of high quality and productivity—if only they will see to it that the plants' managers learn the simple Japanese way.

I am not sure that present conditions are favorable for developing and underdeveloped countries to massively incorporate JIT and TQC concepts in their factories. The Japanese are aggressively setting up subsidiaries in these countries and will surely introduce the concepts. But their diffusion may be slow. Education and information are obstacles in the way of fast diffusion.

Since education (but not information) is an obstacle in the industrialized West as well, the educational obstacle is examined next.

Education and Training

If the Japanese message is that we need to return to simpler ways, what does this portend for our educational institutions? At the

risk of being disemboweled by falling on my own sword (or pow-
dered by falling on my own stick of chalk), I must make some
critical observations on the relevance of business college education and research.

In the United States, business colleges have a major influence upon business enterprise. Many of the top corporations are
run by people with M.B.A. degrees. In short, business management has been professionalized. But with what results?

Educational Commodities

The business (and law) schools provide two commodities: (1)
bright, articulate graduates (they were bright *before* they entered
college; they became articulate in college); (2) business techniques. Both commodities are partly assets, partly liabilities.
Bright graduates are invaluable, but "articulate" can mean fluent
in the jargon of a specialty, which can actually stand in the way
of communication and real problem solving for one's employer.
The purveyors of business techniques—our accountants, management scientists, computer systems analysts, financial managers, lawyers, behavioral scientists, personnel managers, and
market researchers—are all peddling high-cost programs. Being
indirect rather than direct functionaries, they produce no direct
income to the firm, and the amount of their indirect net income is
so difficult to measure that no one knows if the functions are
paying their way.

In visiting Japanese industrial companies, one is struck as
much by the lack of sophisticated techniques, systems, and staff
journeymen as by the productivity of the line organization. In the
face of this evidence from Japan, there is all the more reason
to question the effectiveness of business school education in
the United States, which emphasizes sophisticated techniques
and systems and the supplying of industry with staff journeymen.

Influence of Business Colleges in Japan

Business and industrial managers in Japan are just as likely to hold college degrees as they are in the States. The rigorous college entrance examinations in Japan assure (more than is the case here) that the brightest people get the college degrees. Japanese corporations hiring college graduates therefore obtain bright people, who have become articulate and socially adept during college. Comparatively large numbers of Japanese graduates receive engineering degrees. Others emerge from business studies armed with (and sometimes burdened with) many of the same sophisticated techniques, systems, and programs as are taught in U.S. business schools. (Japanese business college professors, like faculties everywhere, are more apt to teach what is scholarly than what is usable.) Yet those techniques, systems, and programs are not widely used in Japanese industry. Why? The following may partially answer the question.

1. *Numbers*. The ratio of business to engineering graduates is far smaller in Japan than it is here.

2. *M.B.A.'s*. The M.B.A. degree, which can deeply ingrain academic thinking in the minds of its students, is rare in Japan, popular here.

3. *Social structure*. It is imperative for a Japanese graduate to be socially correct, patient, and deferential—behaviors that discourage aggressive promotion of techniques and systems.

4. *Management*. Japanese industrial management techniques evolved in response to the Japanese environmental condition of scarcity and overcrowding and out of the need to correct an image of shoddiness. Simple, direct approaches were affordable—and worked! When the pigeon learns that pecking the target releases a grain of birdseed, the pigeon pecks the target faster and faster. Similarly, Japanese managers, reinforced by success, continue to peck away at the simple and direct sorts of solutions embodied in today's just-in-time and total quality control system.

They say *Hai!* ("Yes") to employees' ideas that are in the same mold, but *Iie* ("No") to complicated, specialist-oriented approaches out of textbooks. Younger employees soon learn which target to peck at. And so Japanese production management improves, with little chance of a major setback arising from a costly complex system that didn't work.

Training a Nation

The whole industrial nation needs to be trained in Japanese techniques. Fortunately, the United States possesses some very effective training institutions capable of leading the effort. The American Production and Inventory Control Society (APICS) and the National Association of Purchasing Management (NAPM) are particularly well organized to spread any new message fast. APICS just completed a highly successful decade-long campaign to train its membership in computer-based material requirements planning, and APICS has already taken some steps to conduct a JIT campaign in the 1980s. The American Management Association, the American Institute of Industrial Engineers, and the American Society for Quality Control are among the many other such organizations that will help spread the word about JIT and TQC. Western Europe does not have so elaborate a network of training-and-development-oriented professional organizations, and so it will probably take longer for European industry to adopt JIT/TQC concepts and techniques.

As good as the U.S. training network is, it cannot compare in effectiveness with the Japanese Union of Scientists and Engineers (JUSE), which has been instrumental in the Japanese quality control movement from the beginning. The deficiency of the American societies is that there are too many of them and they are too specialized, as are the companies where their members are employed. Still, the training task can be accomplished, and in spite of their overemphasis on specialized education, the business colleges probably can help. An asset of America's business colleges is their relatively close associations with industry. Hiring executives as B-school deans is fairly common practice; business schools enroll thousands of working people in evening M.B.A. programs; faculty members conduct a good deal of applied research using real companies as their laboratories; many faculty members do consulting in industry; and most business schools have continuing education and executive development divisions. With such anti–ivory tower activities going on, the business schools usually manage to get involved in whatever industry develops an interest in.

Quality and Productivity in Full Circle

Industry's impending effort to train and tool up to confront Japan's quality and productivity advantage conjures up memories of a similar era over forty years ago. That time the issue was war; this time it is competition. But productivity and quality were industry's chief objectives then as now. It is instructive to consider the initial era's quality/productivity emphasis and its erosion over the years.

Statistical sampling for quality purposes came into being on a large scale in American industry in the 1940s. Military contracts for massive quantities of war matériel demanded their use. Engineers and production managers were industry's glamour boys, and the best minds were employed in the business of increasing productivity. The productivity era continued for several years after the war's end in order to satisfy pent up demands for consumer goods.

Then, rather suddenly in the 1950s the backlogs were depleted, the pipelines were full, and the shelves were stocked. The problem became *over*production and excess capacity. People

214

good at *selling* were in demand, and the marketing era replaced the previous productivity era. Industry's common effort to produce gave way to competition for customers and market share.

But competition is a zero-sum game, with winners and losers. By the 1960s some of the winners had captured enough market share to have become cash cows. Cash presents its own problems: needs for tax shelters, diversifications, acquisition. And, of course, the losers were highly eligible targets for acquisition.

Now the need was not so much for salespeople as for accountants, finance and tax experts, and legal counsel. Accountants could make the balance sheets and income statements look as attractive as possible for firms being taken over, and they could look for tax advantages in the firms doing the acquiring. Equity transfers required financial skills. Lawyers were needed to tie the knot. The financial-legal era of the 1960s had arisen.

Today corporate suites are well stocked with accountants, attorneys, and financiers, most of whom, as is typical of the U.S. system, never held a position in line operations. We have come full circle (see Figure 9–1), back to a need for emphasis on quality and productivity, and our corporations are scrambling to find experienced, talented leaders who have engineering and production experience.

The problem of not having the right skills among our top managers is serious, but what is worse is that our corporations have been controlled by staff specialists for some 30 years. The emphasis on staff has added layers of complex procedures and highly paid indirect employees, and has led to neglect of the revenue-earning end of the business. The kind of highly effective simple systems of enhancing quality and productivity that we may borrow from the Japanese do not fit in easily with such an environment.

We should not think of this state of affairs as being the consequences of errors. Events created needs for marketing expertise in the 1950s and financial-legal expertise in the 1960s—and

215

Figure 9–1. Recent History in American Industry

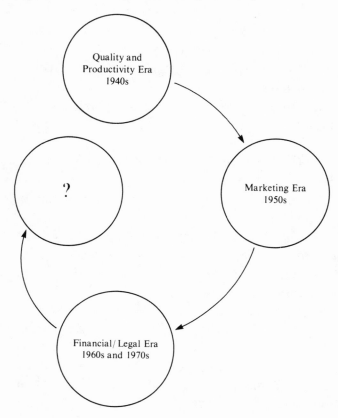

the universities responded magnificently to supply graduates with those skills.

Having come around to a quality/productivity era once more, will we stay with it for only a few years and then recycle through the same series all over again? I think not. The initial cycle was triggered by an aberration, the Second World War. This time international competition provides the impetus for quality and productivity improvement. International competition is unlikely to go away (barring another war), and it creates challenging opportunities requiring new marketing skills as well as financial and legal expertise to form new multinational organizations. In short, the cycle of emphasizing one speciality at a time may have ended, and if so, future needs will be for managers with a healthy mix of types of education and experience.

The point of this discussion is a hopeful one—that in the future we may get steadier and wiser decisions from more broadly based management teams, well represented by people with production backgrounds as well as experience in the staff specialties. This is important for the sake of implementing Japanese systems, because Japanese simplicity is contrary to the tendency of specialists to add more controls and red tape. And more importantly, the marketing, finance, accounting, engineering, and personnel people must be in on the decisions involved in JIT/TQC, since the system entails:

1. Commitment to a marketing and product design strategy featuring fast growth in market share by means of low prices and very high quality of relatively few models, and quick production response to market shifts by means of compressed production lead times and minimal commitment of capacity and inventories to *guesses* about what will sell.

2. Very high inventory turnover (low inventories), a relatively stable work force (facilitated by worker flexibility), capital equipment investments in smaller bites (small, sometimes self-developed, machines), and willingness to suffer several quarters in a row of negative cash flow in times when large numbers of the production workers are performing essential non-revenue-earning tasks like rebuilding production lines. These have important implications for financial planning, personnel administration, and manufacturing engineering.

The JIT/TQC system must not be considered as *just* a production system, because its benefits are clearly strategic and broad.

217

The Time Is Ripe for Change

In this final chapter the prospects for change have been examined. On the negative side are the heavy needs for training and the lack of top people with production experience. But all other factors suggest that U.S. industry (and, to a large extent, all Western industry) is ripe for massive change: top-to-bottom reexamination of objectives, strategies, policies, personnel qualifications, worker training and development, and use of labor— induced by the inability of our present cumbersome systems to compete with the natural state. The Japanese have shown us that even as corporations grow large, the natural state—make a piece, check it, make a piece, check it—can be preserved. The collection of just-in-time and total quality control techniques presented in this book constitute the mechanism that makes such simplicity possible.

In this book I have said a good deal that I know to be true. I have also said things that I infer to be true, and no doubt some of my inferences are dead wrong. Such are the difficulties in examining issues that span nearly global limits in geography, language, and culture. But the gulf between the Far East and the West is not nearly so great as conventional wisdom would have it. I hope this book makes that point.

Finally, the theme of the book and the lesson of this chapter may be restated:

Industry is ready to change its ways, and now we know what to do: Simplify and reduce, simplify and integrate, simplify and expect results.

Appendix: The Kanban System

Kanban (pronounced kahn-bahn), literally translated, means "visible record" or "visible plate." More generally, kanban is taken to mean "card." The Toyota kanban system employs a card to signal the need to *deliver* more parts and an identical or similar card to signal the need to *produce* more parts.

If the kanban system is very loosely interpreted to mean any system employing an order card or delivery card, then most companies all over the world could claim to have one. For example, it has long been standard procedure in industry for a card of some kind to accompany work in process; the card is often known as a "traveler." And a variety of cards or forms—job orders, route sheets, job tickets, and so on—are commonly used in ordering more parts. These traditional cards and visible records do *not* constitute a kanban system, because they are employed in what is known as a *push* system of parts ordering and control. One unique feature of the Toyota kanban system is that it is a *pull* system.

In this appendix the pull vs. push issue is examined, followed by discussion of (1) the full Toyota dual-card kanban system and (2) a popular variation that I am calling single-card kanban. The appendix concludes with comments on kanban vs. computer-based material requirements planning and a few other inventory control systems.

Push or Pull?

For the past 15 years or so, the American Production and Inventory Control Society has provided workshops, expert speakers, and training materials that have found their way into just about every American hamlet that has a manufacturing company. Included in the message being promoted is the view that a well-planned, computer-based *push* system of manufacturing planning and control is the ultimate.

A push system in reality is simply a schedule-based system. That is, a multi-period schedule of future demands for the company's products (called a master production schedule) is prepared, and the computer breaks that schedule down into detailed schedules for making or buying the component parts. It is a push system in that the schedule pushes the production people into making the required parts and then pushing the parts out and onward. The name given to this push system is material requirements planning (MRP).

In the old days before we had the computer power to do all this planning and scheduling, a haphazard pull system was used (and still is in a good many companies). It works as follows: Customers place orders, and manufacturing looks to see if the parts are on hand. Parts not on hand are pulled through, or expedited. Even if substantial amounts of parts are kept on hand, there will be a few missing ones that must be expedited, which is disruptive and keeps customers waiting.

A push/schedule, or MRP, system seems like good management as compared with a pull/expedite system. But a weakness of MRP is that there is some guesswork involved. You need to guess what customer demand will be in order to prepare the schedule, and you need to guess how long it will take your production department to make the needed parts. The system allows corrections to be made daily (called shop-floor control). Nevertheless, bad guesses result in excess inventories of some parts, though not nearly so much total inventory as in the old pull/ expedite system.

Until recently, it appeared that pull systems would gradually be forced out of existence by computer-based MRP, even in small companies, in view of the low and still falling cost of microcomputers. But the Toyota pull system, known as kanban, upsets that prediction. Kanban provides parts when they are needed but without guesswork and therefore without excess inventory resulting from bad guesses. But there is an important limitation to the use of kanban. Kanban will work well only in the context of a just-in-time system in general, and the setup time/lot size reduction feature of JIT in particular. A JIT program can succeed without a kanban subsystem, but kanban makes no sense independently of JIT.

The Toyota Kanban System

In the Toyota kanban system every component part type, or part number, has its own special container designed to hold a precise quantity of the part number, preferably a very small quantity. There are two cards, henceforth referred to as kanban, for each container; and the kanban identify the part number and container capacity, and provide certain other information. One kanban, the production kanban, serves the work center producing the part number; the other, called a conveyance kanban, serves the using work center.[1] Each container cycles from the producing work center and its stock point to the using work center and its stock point, and back, and one kanban is exchanged for the other along the way.

Figure A–1 demonstrates the kanban and container flow pattern for two work centers: a milling work center supplying, say, milled heads to a drilling work center that drills bolt holes in the

Figure A–1. Dual-Card Kanban Flows

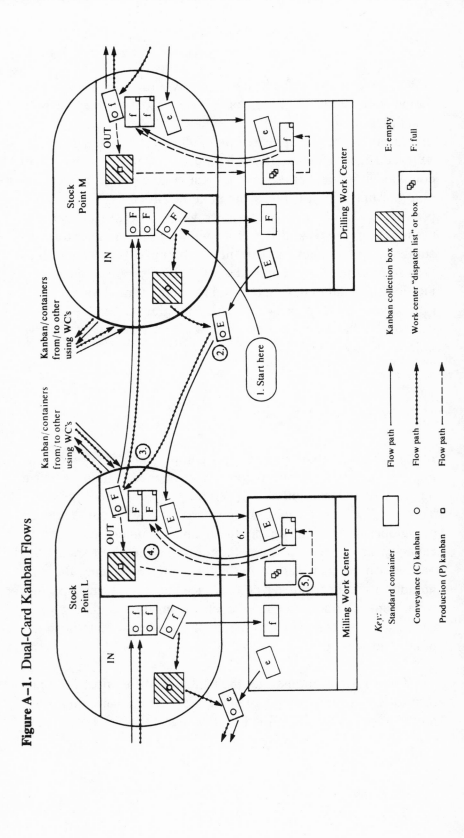

heads. Stock Point L serves Milling (and other nearby work centers); Stock Point M serves Drilling (and other nearby work centers). The flows of parts containers and kanban between Milling and Drilling are shown in the figure by arrows and are described next in step-by-step order.

Dual-Card Kanban and Container Flows

The natural starting point in a pull system is with the pulling (using) work center (WC), Drilling in this example. Parts for Drilling are obtained through use of conveyance kanban (C-kanban), as follows:

1. On Figure A–1, find the note "Start here," pointing to a full parts container about to be moved into Drilling. Its C-kanban is detached and placed in a collection box for Stock Point M.

2. The container most recently emptied in Drilling is taken to Stock Point M, where a C-kanban is attached to it.

3. The empty container and C-kanban are taken to Stock Point L (in another part of the plant or another building), where the C-kanban is detached and reattached to a full container, which is taken back to Stock Point M. The last act also triggers production activities through use of a production kanban (P-kanban), as follows:

4. The full container just taken had a P-kanban attached to it. Before it leaves Stock Point L, its P-kanban is detached and placed in a collection box.

5. P-kanban (that apply to Milling) are taken to Milling every hour or so, where they go into the dispatch box and become the dispatch list of jobs to be worked on next. They are worked on in the order of receipt from Stock Point L.

223

6. Parts for each completed job go into an empty container taken from Stock Point L, the P-kanban is attached, and the full container is moved to Stock Point L.

Rules

The kanban system's simplicity and effectiveness are intertwined in the follwing rules:

1. No parts may be made in Milling unless there is a P-kanban authorizing it. Milling comes to a halt rather than making parts not yet asked for—a pure pull system. (Workers may do maintenance or work on improvement projects when there are no P-kanban in the dispatch box.)

2. There are precisely one C-kanban and one P-kanban for each container, and the number of containers (with kanban) per part number in the system is a carefully considered management decision.

3. Only standard containers may be used, and they always are filled with the prescribed (small) quantity—no more, no less. With such careful control of quantities per container, as well as number of containers per part number, inventory control is simple and far more precise than manual or computer-based Western systems.

Kanban as a Productivity Improvement System

Rule 2 above notes that number of containers is a carefully considered management decision. Too many containers mean too much inventory in the system. In Western thinking too few containers mean too little inventory in the system; not so in the Toyota system. Chapter 2 explained the extraordinary Japanese

224

concept of deliberately removing buffer inventory (or labor) in order to experience—and solve—problems. Use of kanban offers ideal conditions for carrying out the buffer removal tactic. The foreman only needs to remove kanban from the system. Removing kanban is sufficient, because an empty container without kanban attached is ignored and gathers dust. As an illustration of the effects of kanban removal, we may return to the example of Milling and Drilling from Figure A–1.

Let us assume that the process is stable and that there are five kanban in the system; that means five C-kanban, five P-kanban, and five containers of milled heads. Now the shop foreman who supervises both work centers cuts the inventory to four kanban. The likely effect is that Milling will experience its normal problems, and at bad times of the day will have trouble keeping up with Drilling. For example, in a certain two-hour period Milling might find that some of its newly milled heads do not meet specifications, perhaps because of worn bearings in a milling machine, or because of tool wear; a minor accident might send a machinist to the dispensary for first-aid; a machine might break down; small variations in dimensions of the heads to be milled might cause setup delays. Such events slow down Milling's rate of output, perhaps enough so that Drilling uses up three full containers of heads and is idled while Milling completes the order to fill the fourth container. At the end of the day both Drilling and Milling might be behind schedule, which is apparent in two ways.

1. P-kanban and empty containers for certain models have piled up—not a good way to start up production the next day.

2. A count of the day's production—perhaps just a simple totaling of tally marks on a paper or blackboard, where one tally signifies one kanban of heads milled—reveals underproduction. That is, the daily schedule, expressed either by model or as the total of all models, has not been met. For these kinds of parts— milled heads and drilled heads—it is likely that the daily schedule for making the parts would exactly match the daily schedule for the manufacturer's end product, which might be engines. The

foreman generally would direct the two work centers to work overtime until the day's schedule is met.[2]

Workers, group leaders, and the foreman are not pleased about failing to meet the schedule, and most would rather not have unplanned overtime thrust on them. They are, on the other hand, pleased to have unearthed a new set of problems to attack. In the kanban and just-in-time system, workers are always gathering data on the next set of problems, and they are showered with praise periodically when a problem is solved. To earn praise, to avert criticism, to gain self-satisfaction, and to avoid unplanned overtime, kanban workers generally are supportive and enthusiastic about the productivity improvement features of the system.

Of course, the causes of the problems unearthed must be carefully recorded for later analysis by the group, who may be given some company time on certain days of the week for improvement projects. In the above example of milling problems, some possible solutions, stopgap measures, and corrective actions might include:

- Seek management approval to establish a formal project team to study the problem of milled heads not meeting specifications.

- Ask maintenance to investigate machine breakdowns; provide maintenance with the latest breakdown data.

- Place a first-aid kit in the shop for the very minor injuries.

- Get quality control involved in the problem of small variations in dimensions of the heads, so that the problem may be traced to its source.

Limitations of Kanban

Kanban is feasible in just about any plant that makes goods in whole (discrete) units (but not in the process industries). It is beneficial only in certain circumstances:

226

1. Kanban should be an element of a JIT system. It makes little sense to use a pull system if it takes interminably long to pull the necessary parts from the producing work center, as it would if setup times took hours and lot sizes were large. The central feature of JIT is cutting setup times and lot sizes, which allows for fast "pulls" of parts from producing work centers.

2. The parts included in the kanban system should be used every day. Kanban provides for at least one full container of a given part number to be on hand all the time, which is not much inventory idleness if the full container is used up the same day it is produced. Therefore, companies with a kanban system generally apply it to the high-use part numbers, but replenish low-use items by means of conventional Western techniques (e.g., MRP or reorder point).

3. Very expensive or large items should not be included in kanban. Such items are costly to store and carry. Therefore their ordering and delivery should be regulated very closely under the watchful eye of a planner or buyer.

There are numerous fine points that could be made about the Toyota dual-card kanban system. The interested reader will find several sources in English that explain Toyota kanban in more detail.[3] What has not been reported on elsewhere is a popular simplification of kanban, which I am calling single-card kanban, discussed next.

Single-Card Kanban

The number of Japanese companies that have implemented the complete Toyota dual-card kanban system is rather small. Yet there are probably hundreds that claim to have a kanban system. What most of those hundreds have is a single-card kanban system, and the single card that they use is a conveyance kanban (C-kanban). It is easy to begin with a C-kanban system, and then add P-kanban later if it seems beneficial.

227

In single-card kanban, parts are produced and bought according to a daily schedule, and deliveries to the user are controlled by C-kanban. In effect, the single-card system is a push system for production coupled with a pull system for deliveries.

Figure A–2 demonstrates this, using the same example of two work centers, Milling and Drilling, as was used earlier to explain dual-card kanban, shown schematically in Figure A–1. An obvious difference between Figures A–2 and A–1 is that A–2 does not employ a stock point for incoming parts. Instead, parts are delivered right to the point of use in Drilling. Also, the stock point for parts just produced tends to be larger than that for dual-card kanban. The reason for the enlarged stock point is that it holds stock produced to a schedule; the schedule pushes milled parts into the stock point even when Drilling has been slowed or halted as a result of production or quality problems. So the stock point must be able to hold more containers of parts than in the pull system of Figure A–1. The flow of C-kanban and containers is explained next.

Single-Card Kanban and Container Flows

1. Beginning with "Start here" in Figure A–2, we see that a container has just been emptied, and workers have begun to use milled heads from a full container that was "on deck." When the first container was emptied, a worker placed its C-kanban in the kanban collection box.

2. Every half hour or so, an employee (probably in a small delivery vehicle or forklift truck) makes a circuit past all kanban collection boxes in a given plant or area, dropping off full containers and C-kanban from the previous circuit and picking up C-kanban from the boxes. The action taken at number 2 in Figure A–2 is to attach the C-kanban to a full container of milled heads and deliver it to Drilling.

228

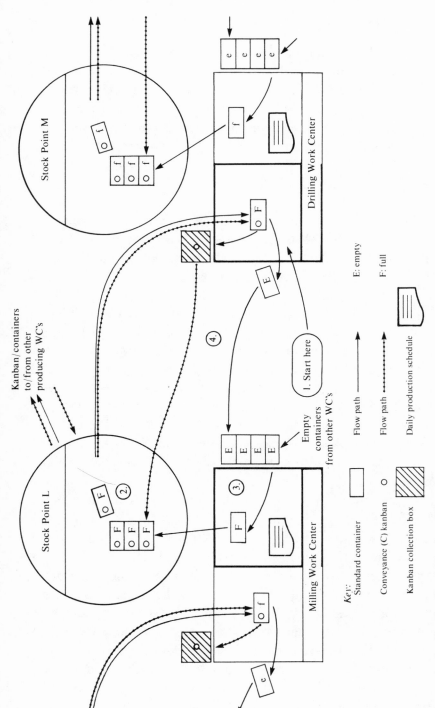

Figure A–2. Single-Card Kanban Flows

Kanban/containers to/from other producing WC's

Stock Point M

Stock Point L

Drilling Work Center

Milling Work Center

Empty containers from other WC's

1. Start here

E: empty
F: full

Key:
Standard container
Conveyance (C) kanban
Kanban collection box

Flow path ————
Flow path • • • • •
Daily production schedule

3. Milling keeps Stock Point L supplied with full containers. Production is tied to a daily schedule, and normally the schedule calls for rotating from model to model during the day.

4. Empty containers are collected periodically from using work centers and taken to producing work centers.

Single-Card Compared with Dual-Card Kanban

Single-card kanban controls deliveries very tightly, so that the using work center never has more than a container or two of parts, and the stock point serving the using work center is eliminated. Relieving the clutter and confusion around points of use is thus an advantage.

On the other hand, produced parts are allowed to build up to some excess in the stock point serving the producing work center. But the buildup need not be serious in companies in which it is relatively easy to associate the required quantity and timing of component parts with the schedule of end products. Examples abound: motorcycles; motors, pumps, and generators; consumer appliances; toys. Compare, for example, a motorcycle plant with an automobile plant. Perhaps the motorcycle plant makes eight sizes in three colors, and type A always takes a type-A frame, type-A engine, type-A fenders, and so forth; there are only a few customer options. Therefore, if the assembly schedule calls for 20 type A's to be completed per day, then 20 fenders per day are needed at, say, minus one hour (one hour prior to completion of each assembly); 20 engines and frames per day are needed at perhaps minus two hours; and so forth. Tube pieces for frames might be punched out at minus one and a half days, but since the tubing then goes through frame welding and painting, where problems and delays can occur, the frame completion schedule might be set at minus two days. The extra half day provides small buffer stocks of tube pieces, completed frames, and painted frames. Single-card kanban nicely controls deliveries of parts from one stage to the next; and the daily parts schedules, appropriately offset for lead time, provide the parts when needed, with rather small inventory buildups.

In comparison with the motorcycle plant, the automobile plant would have maybe ten times as many parts and colors, hundreds of customer choices, and many more stages of production. Compared with motorcycles, there is a far greater potential for delay, which is the compound effect of: (1) large numbers of parts, (2) variable usage of the parts, and (3) multiple stages of manufacture. Daily schedules for producing each part number would have to provide for sizeable buffer stocks (by means of extreme back-scheduling) in order to avoid running out of parts when the delays are bad. Toyota's ingenious solution to the problem is dual-card kanban, which signals production of each part number to match the up-and-down output rate of succeeding production stages.

Dual-card kanban is doubly effective in that it has the productivity improvement feature of removing kanban to expose and solve problems. Unfortunately, single-card kanban cannot employ that feature, because there is no control on number of full containers of a given part number. Therefore, companies that use single-card kanban must get their productivity improvements in some other way. For example, Kawasaki, a single-card company, gets productivity improvements by removing workers from final assembly until yellow lights come on signifying problems in need of correction (see Chapter 4). Nihon Radiator Co., also a single-card user, has a vigorous total quality control system, which features a continual succession of improvement projects; the improvement projects that deal with quality, work methods, tools, or equipment improve productivity by reducing material and labor per unit and by improving equipment and tool utilization.

Is Single-Card Kanban Unique?

I have explained single-card kanban to American managers on a few occasions, and someone usually offers the perceptive comment that "it looks like the old two-bin system to me." The two-bin system is a visual reorder-point technique: When you see that the supply of a part number is down to where you must open the last box (or dip into the second bin), you reorder. Single-card kanban does indeed work that way. It is unique only as an element in a just-in-time system, including but not limited to the following:

1. Standard containers are used.

2. The quantity per container is exact, so that inventory is easy to count and control.

3. The number of full containers at the point of use is only one or two.

4. The quantity in the container is small so that at least one container and usually several containers are used up daily.

5. At the producing end, the containers are filled in small lot sizes, which requires prior action to cut setup times and thereby make small lots economical.

A related question is: What is the significance of the C-kanban? The answer is that the C-kanban is merely an identification card and a convenient signal to bring more parts. There are other effective ways to signal the need for more. As was mentioned in an earlier chapter, one Kawasaki work center conveys the message by rolling a colored golf ball down a pipe to the producing work center; the color identifies the desired part number. At Mitsuboshi Belting Co., scannable computer cards serve as C-kanban; when more parts are needed an on-line scanning device may send a message to a producing work center (or to inventory control). A telephone or intercom could be used—or even a yell, if the producing work center is within earshot.

And, finally, the system could be modified slightly so that the empty container itself signals the need for more parts. Master Lock Corp., an American company, has had such a container-signaling system for making more parts for its locks for over 35 years[4] (but without JIT attributes 1–5 listed above). The necessary modification in a container-signaling system is strict control of number of empty containers; extra empties cannot be sitting around out on the floor, or somebody will assume that they must be filled.

So far in this appendix, dual- and single-card kanban have been explained, and the factor that determines which to adopt has been discussed. That crucial factor is *ease of associating requirements for parts with the schedule of end products.* Actually, we have only examined two degrees of "ease." If it is extremely difficult to associate needs for parts with end-product schedules, then neither type of kanban is very good. Well-known Western inventory systems may be better. A full range of systems is considered next.

Kanban and Other Inventory Systems

The oldest and most widely used inventory system in the world is the reorder-point system (ROP). The simple reorder-point rule is: When stocks get low, order more. Even squirrels follow the rule in replenishing stocks of nuts. But ROP results in high inventories. More parts and raw materials are ordered for the sake of the rule rather than because of need. Manufacturers that use ROP do so because of a difficulty in associating parts requirements with the schedule of end products—the crucial factor mentioned above.

Material requirements planning (MRP) provides a better way. MRP harnesses the computer to perform thousands of simple calculations in transforming a master schedule of end products into parts requirements. But MRP shares one weakness with ROP: It is lot-oriented. That is, in the MRP process the computer collects all demands for a given part number in a given time period, and recommends production or purchase of the part number in one sizeable *lot*. MRP companies order in lots, rather than piece-for-piece (just-in-time), because American MRP companies have not lowered setup times in order to make small lots economical. If they did so, then simple manual kanban rather than complex, expensive, computer-based MRP would be the logical choice. The MRP paradox is that if the company removes the setup time obstacle in order to make MRP truly effective in cutting inventories to the bone, then MRP is no longer needed; kanban is preferable.

The point may be stated in terms of the "crucial factor": MRP correctly calculates parts requirements by precisely associating them with the master schedule of end products. But what is correct at the time of calculation is subject to error later. The reason is that lots are sizeable, and the production lead time is long, from one to several weeks. During that lead time there will be delays and schedule changes so that the lot being produced no longer is correct in relation to the master schedule of end products. The lot size and lead time erode the close association between parts requirements and end-product schedules.

The four inventory systems discussed in this chapter—single-card kanban, dual-card kanban, MRP, and ROP—seem to fall naturally onto a continuum. Figure A–3 shows those four cases plus one more, the continuous system, on the extreme left. What Figure A–3 shows is that as it becomes harder to associate parts and end-product demands, inventories are likely to increase—from theoretical zero on the extreme left to months' worth on the extreme right. We may separately consider each of the five inventory systems that constitute this continuum.

Weeks' or months' worth of inventory is typical of the reorder-point (ROP) system (type 5), which is the dominant system in companies that experience large delays (lead time) between parts manufacture and parts use. Some companies, especially small job shops, deliberately position themselves in a market whose customers are buying variety and the manufacturer's flexibility.

234

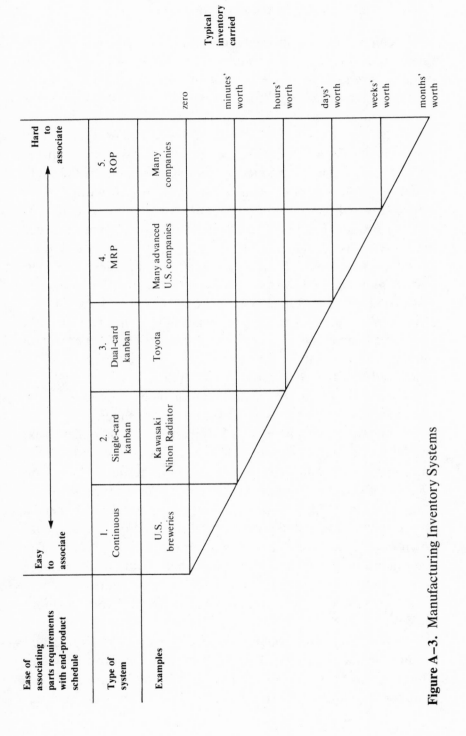

Figure A–3. Manufacturing Inventory Systems

Such companies cannot schedule accurately in advance and therefore resort to high inventories replenished through ROP. If products are rather complex (involving multiple stages of manufacture), inventories will build further because of buffer stock between stages.

Days' or weeks' worth of materials is typical for type-4 companies in the figure: the MRP companies, mostly found in the United States. These producers are able to shuck off the high-inventory ROP system, because they are blessed with or have forged (through better management) a closer link between parts and end-product demands, which makes future scheduling of end products realistic. Such companies may have less variety (i.e., by selling fewer models) than the type-5 companies, and their market may demand faster deliveries; but production is in lots, and a produced lot often covers demands for a week or more.[5]

Days' or hours' worth of materials is shown for the Toyota dual-card kanban system, type 3 in Figure A–3. Further reduction in variety (number of models), plus engineering to cut setup times, reduces the delay from parts manufacture to parts use—and cuts lot sizes to approach piece-for-piece production. The manufacturing process has become more streamlined.

Companies using single-card kanban, type 2, like Kawasaki and Nihon Radiator, have still less delay or lead time between parts production and use. Companies may be in that situation because of very few models, few levels of manufacture, the manufacture of everything from only a few raw materials, a concerted attack upon sources of delay (setup delays, quality delays, breakdown delays, worker delays), and perhaps other reasons. The manufacturing process has been simplified or streamlined to the point where inventory could be cut to perhaps minutes' worth in some cases, if the effort was made, but hours' worth is more typical.

Type-1 companies have fully streamlined plants with each production line dedicated to one model. The goods flow like water without stops for inventory buildup, so that the minimum of zero inventory is imaginable. American breweries are not quite continuous producers since the liquid goes into cans, kegs, and bottles (discrete units). But the lead time from empty to full can is very short, so that the canning schedule may nearly serve as the delivery schedule for incoming empties. According to one report,[6] Anheuser-Busch, Inc., unloads a nearly continuous stream of trucks bringing in empties, and uses them soon enough that the average inventory of unfilled cans is only two hours.

In Figure A–3, type 1 is called a "continuous" system, which in this case refers to the nature of the flow of materials and not the system for controlling the flow. Actually, when a company enjoys such a degree of streamlined flow, just about any inventory system will keep inventories low—even reorder-point. At Matsushita Electric's highly automated refrigerator plant at Lake Biwa, reorder-point is used; inventories are low but could probably be worked down quite a bit lower if there were significant savings to be had from doing so. But bigger savings lie elsewhere. The point is that manufacturers that are type 1 need not worry about inventories much, and type-2 firms are somewhat the same, so their inventory systems are usually simple. Type 3 and 4 companies have huge potential inventories to be concerned about, and their inventory systems therefore receive great attention. Type-5 companies have the greatest inventory problems, and indeed they often fail because of inability to finance the inventory burden. They either must develop into type 4 or 3 companies or must stay healthy by providing unique products or services.

Is Western Industry Ready for Kanban?

The answer to the question in the heading is a qualified no. Mostly, Western companies do not have the prerequisite conditions for kanban to be useful. Western brewers, bottlers, and canners are too much like process industries to use kanban, which is a technique oriented toward discrete, not continuous, processes. Western companies using reorder-point or material requirements planning could adopt single-card or dual-card kanban, but they would not gain any just-in-time benefits in so doing. The first steps must be to cut lot sizes through setup-time engineering and to streamline the plant configuration. A sound TQC program to reduce quality-related delays, stoppages, and rework will also reduce the lead time and bring the demand for parts into closer sync with demand for end products.

When such preparations have been completed, some MRP companies may find it natural to adopt single-card kanban. MRP perhaps would be retained for scheduling—the push system— and C-kanban would be used to pull the parts from producing to using work centers.

Some MRP companies, especially those with multiple levels of processing, may evolve to type-3 companies—resembling Toyota in regard to ease of associating parts demand with end-product demand schedules. In that case, MRP could be retained for capacity-planning purposes, and dual-card kanban adopted for pulling parts through the manufacturing processes. Yamaha Motor Corp. has developed a halfway system that marries MRP to dual-card kanban; Yamaha calls it *synchro-MRP*.[7] Perhaps synchro-MRP is the best choice for some Western MRP companies that are able to evolve leftward along the continuum of Figure A–3.

Finally, Western ROP companies that are able to streamline their processing and reduce the uncertainty of the coupling between parts and end-product schedules often will want to bypass the MRP stage. MRP is a very expensive undertaking, and its approach is to attack problems with complex solutions, i.e., computer systems. Where there are many stages of production, MRP or synchro-MRP may be necessary. In most cases, however, money is better spent on JIT/TQC than on computer-based planning and control. If we have learned anything from the Japanese, it is that simplification is generally the safest path to improvement.

238

Notes

Preface (pp. vii–x)

1. Michael E. McGill, "Z and the Seven S's: A Modern Management Fable," *The Collegiate Forum* (Fall 1981), pp. 2–3.

Chapter 1: Industrial Management in Japan and the World (pp. 1–14)

1. Homer Dansby, "Evolution of Japanese Production Control Systems," presentation at seminar entitled " 'Made in Japan': The Formula for Success," sponsored by Arthur Andersen and Co. and the Kansas City chapter of the American Production and Inventory Control Society (Kansas City, April 25, 1981).

2. My sources include: Robert E. Fox, "Keys to Successful Materials Management Systems: A Contrast Between Japan, Europe and the U.S.," *National Conference Proceedings, American Production and Inventory Control Society* (Boston, October 6–9, 1981), pp. 322–326; and Dick Leising of IBM, Minneapolis office, dinner speaker at the Great Plains chapter of the American Production and Inventory Control Society (Lincoln, October 23, 1980).

3. The American Production and Inventory Control Society's concerted effort to educate industry on MRP has frequently been called the "MRP crusade."

Chapter 2: Just-in-Time Production with Total Quality Control (pp. 15–45)

1. Robert W. Hall, "Driving the Productivity Machine: Production Planning and Control in Japan" (Falls Church, Va.: American Production and Inventory Control Society, Fall 1981), p. 13.

2. Y. Sugimori, K. Kusunoki, F. Cho, and S. Uchikawa, "Toyota Production System and Kanban System—Materialization of Just-in-Time and Respect-

for-Human System," *International Journal of Production Research,* Vol. 15, No. 6 (1977), pp. 553–64.

3. Yasuhiro Monden, "How Toyota Shortened Supply Lot Production Time, Waiting Time, and Conveyance Time," *Industrial Engineering* (September 1981), pp. 22–30.

4. Hall, *op. cit.,* p. 13.

5. "Report of the Production Management for Small Industries Study Mission to Japan from the Republic of China" (Asian Productivity Center, December 4–17, 1968), p. 6.

6. Recently General Motors launched its own Japanese-style buying program, which calls for daily deliveries "just in time" for use in production. See "GM Spreads the Misery," *Newsweek* (April 5, 1982), p. 54.

7. The metaphor has been visually depicted in a slide presentation that has been shown to audiences around the country by Leighton Smith, an Arthur Andersen and Co. consultant who was on assignment in Japan for five years.

8. Presentation by W. Earl Sasser, in session on "Teaching Productivity and Quality in a Business Curriculum," national conference of the American Institute for Decision Sciences (Boston, November 18–20, 1981).

9. A mathematically correct learning curve formula to express the same thing is cumbersome: $V = C^x$, where x is the exponent, $\dfrac{1}{(\log 2/3)/(\log 2)}$.

10. The Western ear can scarcely distinguish between *muda* and *mura,* even if correctly pronounced.

Chapter 3: Total Quality Control (pp. 47–82)

1. A. V. Feigenbaum, *Total Quality Control: Engineering and Management* (New York: McGraw-Hill, 1961), p. 17.

2. J. M. Juran, "Product Quality—a Prescription for the West. Part I: Training and Improvement Programs," *Management Review,* Vol. 70, No. 6 (June 1981), pp. 8–14.

3. "Small Sawmill Survives by Setting Its Blades for Exports to Japan," *The Wall Street Journal* (May 7, 1981), pp. 1, 14.

4. Ikuro Kusaba, "Quality Control in Japan." "Reports of QC Circle Activities," No. 14, Union of Japanese Scientists and Engineers (1981), pp. 1–5.

5. "Sanyo Manufacturing Corporation—Forrest City, Arkansas," Harvard Business School, case number 2–682–045 (1981).

6. Yasuhiro Monden, "What Makes the Toyota Production System Really Tick?" *Industrial Engineering* (January 1981), pp. 36–46.

7. Yoshi Tsurumi, "Productivity: The Japanese Approach," *Pacific Basin Quarterly,* No. 6 (Summer 1981), p. 8.

8. J. M. Juran, "Japanese and Western Quality: A Contrast in Methods and Results," *Management Review* (November 1978), pp. 26–45.

9. Tsurumi, *op. cit.*, p. 7.

10. "Sanyo," Harvard case 2–682–045, *op. cit.*

11. Tsurumi, *op. cit.*, p. 8.

12. "Sanyo," Harvard case 2–682–045, *op. cit.*, p. 5.

13. Juran, "Product Quality—a Prescription for the West," *Management Review* (June 1981), *op. cit.*

14. Philip B. Crosby, *Quality Is Free: The Art of Making Quality Certain* (New York: McGraw-Hill, 1979).

15. William M. Ringle, "The American Who Remade 'Made in Japan,'" *Nation's Business* (February 1981), p. 69.

Chapter 4: The Debut of Just-in-Time Production in the United States (pp. 83–102)

1. Robert W. Hall (ed.), "Kawasaki, U.S.A.: Transferring Japanese Production Methods to the United States: A Case Study" (Falls Church, Va.: American Production and Inventory Control Society, 1981).

2. An early English-language source was Y. Sugimori, K. Kusunoki, F. Cho, and S. Uchikawa, "Toyota Production System and Kanban System: Materialization of Just-in-Time and Respect-for-Human System," *International Journal of Production Research,* Vol. 15, No. 6 (1977), pp. 553–564.

3. No attempt has been made to ascertain whether Butt, or perhaps KHI, Japan, was the original source of the plant vision statement or the EOQ charts. Whatever their source, Butt was their enthusiastic purveyor.

4. American overspecialization is a major topic in William Ouchi, *Theory Z: How American Business Can Meet the Japanese Challenge* (Reading, Mass.: Addison-Wesley, 1981).

5. There is research to prove the point and also research to disprove it. But as is often true of such research, the study environments range from Boy Scout groups trying to set up tents and fraternity social committees trying to plan beer busts to professors coauthoring books and corporate executive committees making economic decisions. It is no wonder that the research results are equivocal.

6. Barnard is the respected author of the management classic *The Functions of the Executive* (Cambridge, Mass.: The President and Fellows of Harvard College, 1938).

7. Ed Hay, "Planning to Implement Kanban," presentation to the Repetitive Manufacturing Group of the American Production and Inventory Control Society, Just-in-Time Workshop (Lincoln, Neb., June 11–12, 1981).

8. "How the Japanese Manage in the U.S.," *Fortune* (June 15, 1981), pp. 97–103.

9. Conversation with Robert Summers, consultant and former Kawasaki personnel manager (May 6, 1982).

Chapter 5: Plant Configurations (pp. 103–130)

1. The configurations are adapted from Richard J. Schonberger, Doug Sutton, and Jerry Claunch, "Kanban (Just-in-Time) Applications at Kawasaki, U.S.A.," *National Conference Proceedings, American Production and Inventory Control Society* (Boston, October 6–9, 1981), pp. 188–191.

2. For example, John L. Burbidge, *The Introduction of Group Technology* (New York: Wiley/Halstead, 1975).

3. "Japanese Push Robots," *Datamation* (July 1980), pp. 56–57.

4. Urban C. Lehner, "Japan Worries About a 'Gray' Future," *The Wall Street Journal* (June 1, 1981), p. 1.

5. Arnold R. Weber, "The Changing Labor Market in the 1980s," E. J. Faulkner Lecture, College of Business Administration, University of Nebraska–Lincoln (October 7, 1980).

Chapter 6: Production-Line Management
(pp. 131–155)

1. Ray Wild, *Mass-production Management: The Design and Operation of Production Flow-line Systems* (London: Wiley, 1972).

2. William D. Torrence, "Viability of Portions of the Japanese Industrial Relations Model on the Great Plains of the United States: Kawasaki Motors Corporation, Lincoln, Nebraska," unpublished paper, University of Nebraska–Lincoln.

3. "APICS Tours Japan," *Production and Inventory Management Review and APICS News,* Vol. 2, No. 5 (May 1982), p. 7.

4. Wild, *op. cit.,* p. 110.

5. Quoted in W. Earl Sasser, "Quality: A Presentation to the A.I.D.S. Group," unpublished summarization of materials presented at the national conference of the American Institute for Decision Sciences (Boston: November 18–20, 1981).

6. Wild, *op. cit.,* p. 177.

7. The remarks in this paragraph are attributable to Ed Hay of Fram Corp., who spent three weeks in Japan thoroughly studying Toyota and its suppliers. In my own visit to Japan, I found that the idea has spread to other OEM companies and supplier plants, whose managers showed me their own examples of U-shaped work areas.

8. Theodore O. Prenting and Nicholas T. Thomopoulos, *Humanism and Technology in Assembly Line Systems* (Rochelle Park, N.J.: Spartan Books, 1974), p. 209.

9. There is a body of scholarly writings, in English, on mixed-model sequencing that applies, e.g.: Wild, *op. cit.,* Chapter 7; and Prenting and Thomopoulos, *op. cit.,* Chapter 14.

10. Monden says much the same thing but expressed as a general principle: "If the subsequent process withdraws materials in a fluctuating manner in regards to time and quantity, then the preceding processes should prepare as much inventory, equipment and manpower as needed to adapt to the peak in the variance of quantities demanded": Yasuhiro Monden, "What Makes the Toyota Production System Really Tick?" *Industrial Engineering* (January 1981), pp. 36–46.

Chapter 7: Just-in-Time Purchasing (pp. 157–179)

1. Wickham Skinner, "The Focused Factory," *Harvard Business Review* (May–June 1974), pp. 113–121.

2. William J. Abernathy, Kim B. Clark, and Alan M. Kantrow, "The New Industrial Strategy," *Harvard Business Review* (September–October 1981), pp. 68–81.

3. "Auto Makers Have Trouble with 'Kanban,' " *The Wall Street Journal* (April 7, 1982), pp. 1, 32.

4. "GM Spreads the Misery," *Newsweek* (April 5, 1982), pp. 54–55.

5. "GM's Changes in Buying Steel Upset Industry," *The Wall Street Journal* (May 6, 1982), p. 27.

6. Jeremy Main, "The Battle for Quality Begins," *Fortune* (December 29, 1980), pp. 28–33.

Chapter 8: Quality Circles, Work Improvement, and Specialization (pp. 181–198)

1. Robert H. Hayes, "Why Japanese Factories Work," *Harvard Business Review* (July–August 1981), pp. 57–66.

2. "Oriental Hospitality: Japanese Factories Are Points of Interest to Foreign Tourists Studying Technology," *The Wall Street Journal* (September 3, 1981), p. 40.

3. Christopher S. Gray, "Total Quality Control in Japan—Less Inspection, Lower Cost," *Business Week* (July 16, 1981), pp. 23–44.

4. J. M. Juran, "Product Quality—a Prescription for the West," *Management Review,* Vol. 70, No. 7 (July 1981), pp. 57–61.

5. Robert E. Cole, "Learning from the Japanese: Prospects and Pitfalls," *Management Review* (September 1980), pp. 22–28.

6. Ikuro Kusaba, "Quality Control in Japan," in "Reports of QC Circle Activities," No. 14, Union of Japanese Scientists and Engineers (1981), pp. 1–5.

Notes

7. William G. Ouchi, *Theory Z: How American Business Can Meet the Japanese Challenge* (Reading, Mass.: Addison-Wesley, 1981), p. 33.

8. Peter F. Drucker, "Getting Control of Corporate Staff Work," *The Wall Street Journal* (April 28, 1981), p. 24.

9. Arch Patton, "Industry's Misguided Shift to Staff Jobs," *Business Week* (April 5, 1981), pp. 12–13.

10. Sadakazu Shindo, "Conditions for Activating a Corporation," part 4 of a 6-part series, *The Oriental Economist* (July 1981), pp. 38–43.

11. "A New Target: Reducing Staff and Levels," *Business Week* (December 21, 1981), pp. 69–73.

12. "Kaiser Aluminum Flattens Its Layers of Brass," *Business Week* (February 24, 1973), pp. 81–82.

13. Robert Townsend, *Up the Organization* (New York: Knopf, 1970).

14. For the fun of it, I once formulated the viewpoint into "Schonberger's Law of Effectiveness": The effectiveness of an activity is inversely proportional to its distance away from the primary mission.

Chapter 9: Prospects for Catching Up (pp. 199–218)

1. William G. Ouchi, *Theory Z: How American Business Can Meet the Japanese Challenge* (Reading, Mass.: Addison-Wesley, 1981).

2. Richard Tanner Pascale and Anthony G. Athos, *The Art of Japanese Management: Applications for American Executives* (New York: Simon & Schuster, 1981).

3. Ezra F. Vogel, *Japan as Number 1: Lessons for America* (New York: Harper & Row [Colophon], 1979), pp. 76–78.

4. "Many U.S. Exporters Compete Successfully, Especially in Europe," *The Wall Street Journal* (December 21, 1981), pp. 1, 10.

5. "How the Japanese Manage in the U.S.," *Fortune* (June 15, 1981), pp. 97–103.

6. Sadakazu Shindo, "Conditions for Activating a Corporation," part 4 of a 6-part series, *The Oriental Economist* (July 1981), pp. 38–43.

Appendix: The Kanban System (pp. 219–238)

1. There are a variety of other special types of kanban used by Toyota, but most are variations of these two. For further information, see Yasuhiro Monden, "Adaptable Kanban System Helps Toyota Maintain Just-in-Time Production," *Industrial Engineering* (May 1981), pp. 29–46.

2. Japanese overtime policies vary in pay, number of permissible hours per day and per week, etc.; the policy in one company that I visited is no overtime on Wednesday.

3. Robert W. Hall, "Driving the Productivity Machine: Production Planning and Control in Japan (Falls Church, Virginia: American Production and Inventory Control Society, 1981). Monden, *op. cit.* Y. Sugimori, K. Kusunoki, F. Cho, and S. Uchikawa, "Toyota Production System and Kanban System: Materialization of Just-in-Time and Respect-for-Human System," *International Journal of Production Research,* Vol. 15, No. 6 (1977), pp. 553–564.

4. Bob Hintz, of Master Lock Corp., presentation to the Just-in-Time Workshop of the APICS Repetitive Manufacturing Group (Lincoln, Neb., June 11–12, 1981).

5. There is a "type-4½" company that is omitted from Figure A–3 to keep it simple. It is the company that replenishes parts via ROP, and to cope with ROP failures, uses the computer to: (a) explode the bills of materials for the next weeks' master schedule to yield gross parts requirements, (b) deduct on-hand balances, and (c) produce a shortage list for expediting purposes. This is a popular system that I call "ROP/shortage list," and which some people incorrectly refer to as MRP. (It is not MRP, because the computer schedule extends only one period into the future, which obviates advance planning of parts needs.) See Richard J. Schonberger, "The ROP/Shortage List System," *Production and Inventory Management,* Vol. 21, No. 3 (Fall 1980), pp. 106–117.

6. Glen Eisen, Arthur Andersen and Co., speech to Omaha chapter of National Purchasing Management Association (December 9, 1981).

7. Synchro-MRP is explained in Hall, *op. cit.*

Bibliography

ABERNATHY, WILLIAM J.; KIM B. CLARK; and ALAN M. KANTROW. "The New Industrial Strategy." *Harvard Business Review* (September–October 1981), pp. 68–81.

"A New Target: Reducing Staff and Levels." *Business Week* (December 21, 1981), pp. 69–72.

"APICS Tours Japan." *Production and Inventory Management Review and APICS News,* Vol. 2, No. 5 (May 1982), p. 7.

"Auto Makers Have Trouble with Kanban." *The Wall Street Journal* (April 7, 1982), pp. 1, 32.

BURBIDGE, JOHN L. *The Introduction of Group Technology.* New York: Wiley/Halstead, 1975.

COLE, ROBERT E. "Learning from the Japanese: Prospects and Pitfalls." *Management Review* (September 1980), pp. 22–28.

CROSBY, PHILIP B. *Quality is Free: The Art of Making Quality Certain.* New York: McGraw-Hill, 1979.

DEMING, W. EDWARDS. "What Top Management Must Do." *Business Week* (July 20, 1981), pp. 19–21.

DIGMAN, L. A. "Strategic Management in U.S. vs. Japanese Firms." Unpublished paper. University of Nebraska–Lincoln (April 1982).

DRUCKER, PETER. "Getting Control of Corporate Staff Work." *The Wall Street Journal* (April 28, 1981), p. 24.

FEIGENBAUM, A. V. *Total Quality Control: Engineering and Management.* New York: McGraw-Hill, 1961.

FOX, ROBERT E. "Keys to Successful Materials Management Systems: A Contrast Between Japan, Europe and the U.S." *National Conference Proceedings, American Production and Inventory Control Society* (Boston, October 6–9, 1981), pp. 322–326.

FUKUDA, RYUJI. "Introduction to the CEDAC." *Quality Progress* (November 1981), pp. 14–19.

"GM Spreads the Misery." *Newsweek* (April 5, 1982), pp. 54–55.

"GM's Changes in Buying Steel Upset Industry." *The Wall Street Journal* (May 6, 1982), p. 27.

GRAY, CHRISTOPHER S. "Total Quality Control in Japan—Less Inspection, Lower Cost." *Business Week* (July 20, 1981), pp. 23–44.

HALL, ROBERT W. (ed.). "Driving the Productivity Machine: Production Planning and Control in Japan." Falls Church, Va.: American Production and Inventory Control Society, Fall 1981.

———. "Kawasaki, U.S.A.: Transferring Japanese Production Methods to the United States: A Case Study." Falls Church, Va.: American Production and Inventory Control Society, 1981.

———. "Why the Excitement About Repetitive Manufacturing?" *Production and Inventory Management Review and APICS News* (August 1981), pp. 14–18.

HAYES, ROBERT H. "Why Japanese Factories Work." *Harvard Business Review* (July–August 1981), pp. 57–66.

"How the Japanese Manage in the U.S." *Fortune* (June 15, 1981), pp. 97–103.

ISHIKAWA, KAORU. *Guide to Quality Control.* Tokyo: Asian Productivity Organization, 1972.

———. "Quality Control Starts and Ends with Education." *Quality Progress* (August 1972), p. 18.

JURAN, J. M. "Japanese and Western Quality: A Contrast in Methods and Results." *Management Review* (November 1978), pp. 26–45.

———. "Product Quality—a Prescription for the West: Part I: Training and Improvement Programs." *Management Review,* Vol. 70, No. 6 (June 1981), pp. 8–14.

"Kaiser Aluminum Flattens Its Layers of Brass." *Business Week* (February 24, 1973), pp. 81–82.

KRAJEWSKI, LEE J.; BARRY E. KING; LARRY P. RITZMAN; NAN WIENER; and DANNY S. WONG. "A Comparison of Japanese and American Systems for Inventory and Productivity Management: A Simulation Approach." *National Conference Proceedings, American Institute for Decision Sciences* (Boston, November 18–20, 1981), pp. 109–111.

KUSABA, IKURO. "Quality Control in Japan." in "Reports of QC Activities," No. 14, Union of Japanese Scientists and Engineers (1981), pp. 1–5.

LEE, S. M., and GARY SCHWENDIMAN. *Management by Japanese Systems.* New York: Praeger, 1982.

MAIN, JEREMY. "The Battle for Quality Begins." *Fortune* (December 29, 1980), pp. 28–33.

"Many U.S. Exporters Compete Successfully, Especially in Europe." *The Wall Street Journal* (December 21, 1981), pp. 1, 10.

MONDEN, YASUHIRO. "Adaptable Kanban System Helps Toyota Maintain Just-in-Time Production." *Industrial Engineering* (May 1981), pp. 29–46.

———. "Toyota's Production-Smoothing Methods: Part II." *Industrial Engineering* (September 1981), pp. 22–30.

———. "What Makes the Toyota Production System Really Tick?" *Industrial Engineering* (January 1981), pp. 36–46.

"Oriental Hospitality: Japanese Factories Are Points of Interest to Foreign Tourists Studying Technology." *The Wall Street Journal* (September 3, 1981), p. 40.

OUCHI, WILLIAM G. *Theory Z: How American Business Can Meet the Japanese Challenge.* Reading, Mass.: Addison-Wesley, 1981.

PASCALE, RICHARD TANNER, and ANTHONY G. ATHOS. *The Art of Japanese Management: Applications for American Executives.* New York: Simon & Schuster, 1981.

PATTON, ARCH. "Industry's Misguided Shift to Staff Jobs." *Business Week* (April 5, 1981), pp. 12–13.

PRENTING, THEODORE O., and NICHOLAS T. THOMOPOULOS. *Humanism and Technology in Assembly Line Systems.* Rochelle Park, N.J.: Spartan Books, 1974.

"Report of the Production Management for Small Industries Study Mission to Japan from the Republic of China." Asian Productivity Center (December 4–17, 1968).

RINGLE, WILLIAM. "The American Who Remade 'Made in Japan.' " *Nation's Business* (February 1981), pp. 67–70.

"Sanyo Manufacturing Corporation—Forrest City, Arkansas." Harvard Business School, case number 2–682–045 (1981).

SASSER, W. EARL. "Quality: A Presentation to the A.I.D.S. Group." Unpublished summarization of materials presented at the national conference of the American Institute for Decision Sciences (Boston: November 18–20, 1981).

SCHONBERGER, RICHARD J. "A Stage-Developmental Model of Manufacturing Inventory Management Systems." *Southwest AIDS Proceedings* (Dallas, March 18–22, 1982), pp. 169–171.

249

Bibliography

———. "Implementation of Japanese Manufacturing Management in the U.S." *National Conference Proceedings, American Institute for Decision Sciences* (Boston: November 18–20, 1981), pp. 98–99.

———. "Productivity in Full Circle." *P/OM Perspectives,* Vol. 9, No. 1 (Fall 1981), pp. 1–2.

———. "Selecting the Right Manufacturing Inventory System: Western and Japanese Approaches." *Production and Inventory Management* (in press).

———. "Some Observations on the Advantages and Implementation Issues of Just-in-Time Production Systems." *Journal of Operations Management* (Fall 1982).

———. "The Transfer of Japanese Manufacturing Management Approaches to U.S. Industry." *Academy of Management Review* (July 1982).

———; DOUG SUTTON; and JERRY CLAUNCH. "Kanban (Just-in-Time) Applications at Kawasaki, U.S.A." *National Conference Proceedings, American Production and Inventory Control Society* (Boston, October 6–9, 1981), pp. 188–191.

SHINDO, SADAKAZU. "Conditions for Activating a Corporation." 6-part series. *The Oriental Economist* (March through May and July through September 1981).

SKINNER, WICKHAM. "The Focused Factory." *Harvard Business Review* (May–June 1974), pp. 113–121.

"Small Sawmill Survives by Setting Its Blades for Exports to Japan." *The Wall Street Journal* (May 7, 1981), pp. 1, 14.

SMITH, MARTIN R. *Qualitysense.* New York: American Management Association, 1979.

STEPHENS, KENNETH S. "Quality and Quality Control." Productivity Series No. 11. Asian Productivity Organization, 1976.

SUGIMORI, Y.; K. KUSUNOKI; F. CHO; and S. UCHIKAWA. "Toyota Production System and Kanban System: Materialization of Just-in-Time and Respect-for-Human System." *International Journal of Production Research,* Vol. 15, No. 6 (1977), pp. 553–564.

TORRENCE, WILLIAM D. "Viability of Portions of the Japanese Industrial Relations Model on the Great Plains of the United States: Kawasaki Motors Corporation, Lincoln, Nebraska." Unpublished paper. University of Nebraska–Lincoln.

250

TOWNSEND, ROBERT. *Up the Organization*. New York: Knopf, 1970.

TSURUMI, YOSHI. "Productivity: The Japanese Approach." *Pacific Basin Quarterly,* No. 6 (Summer 1981), pp. 7–9.

VOGEL, EZRA F. *Japan as Number 1: Lessons for America*. New York: Harper & Row (Colophon), 1979.

WHEELWRIGHT, STEVEN C. "Japan—Where Operations Really Are Strategic." *Harvard Business Review* (July–August 1981), pp. 67–74.

WILD, RAY. *Mass-production Management: The Design and Operation of Production Flow-line Systems*. London: Wiley, 1972.

Index